ABOU

Retired railroader, Denton Dabbs, was born and raised in Chattanooga, Tennessee. After the Japanese struck Pearl Harbor in December of 1941, he enlisted in the Naval Air Corps and later, the Army Air Corps. Denton was two flights away from graduating Bombardier school when Japan signed their formal surrender. His time in military service,(comma typo in copy) would provide many lasting impression and relationships which are often recalled in columns he writes for the Dade County Sentinel in Trenton, Georgia. Shared Memories is more than the story of one man... it is an intimate look at the service of a generation.

World War II
Shared Memories

by Denton Dabbs

TURNER PUBLISHING COMPANY

Turner Publishing Company

Turner Publishing Company Staff:
Editor: Bill Schiller
Designer: Heather R. Warren

Copyright © 1999
Denton Dabbs
Publishing Rights:
Turner Publishing Company

Library of Congress Catalog
Card No. 99-66067

ISBN: 978-1-68162-399-3

TABLE OF CONTENTS

DEDICATION

This book is dedicated to all those men and women who served their country and helped to preserve the freedom we enjoy today. Permit me to extend a special dedication to some of my personal friends who died in training or in combat.

Aviation Cadet William C. Wheat, killed while in training.
Lt. William C. Williams, Bombardier, shot down over Austria.
Ensign James Campbell, crashed off the coast of Florida.
Victor Culberson, reported killed in action.
Lt. David 0. Schoocraft, reported killed.
Capt. Herbert C. Davis, killed in plane crash in New Mexico.
First Lt. James R. Crockett, P-51 fighter pilot, shot down over Germany.
Lt. Edward T. Wilson, B-26 bomber pilot, shot down over Italy.
Lt. Jack Clark, Bombardier, shot down over Germany.
Lt. T. E. Hale, fighter pilot, killed in a crash in England.
First Lt. Kenneth D. Hicks, shot down over Germany.
Staff Sgt. Sam B. Henry, killed in Belgium.
Staff Sgt. Lawrence S. Medlin, killed in a bomber crash in Arizona.
First Lt. Travis Moore, bomber pilot, shot down over Truk in the Pacific.
Lt. Roy E. Thomas, pilot, last reported on Corregidor and Bataan.

For pictures of the men listed above, please see the memorial section beginning on page 140.

FOREWORD

When I was a small boy in the 1920's, our town had a Veterans Day each year for the remaining veterans from the Civil War. I was always impressed to see these old men as they marched down the street. Most of them had long beards and wore their tattered old uniforms. Some hobbled along on a peg leg. It was not long until that generation of men had passed and eventually, they were all gone.

As I grew into manhood, I often thought what a shame that I had not been old enough to talk at length with some of those old veterans and record their stories.

My generation was caught up in World War II, but now, we are entering our twilight years. These are the stories of some of those men who trained for tasks they never dreamed they would be doing, who went to places they had never even heard of before, and accomplished feats they scarcely imagined possible. The stories are true and when combined, they represent a portion of our shared memories from a most significant era of world history.

JUNE 6, 1944

When I was a youngster in school we were taught that there were a great many dates in history that were important to remember. We were always being asked to memorize certain dates like the discovery of America in 1492, the settlement of the first colony at Jamestown, Va. in 1607, and on and on.

Everyone, of course, remembers family birth dates, anniversary dates and possibly other special events. Beyond these, however, there are two dates that will always remain in my memory and perhaps in the memory of all those from my generation.

On December 7, 1941 the Japanese bombed Pearl Harbor and we were drawn into World War II. I was a young man of 21, just a few days short of my 22nd birthday, and I will always remember that day in December.

The world would change in those next few years and none of us knew where we would go or what part we would play. The uncertainty of those days was staggering for the young people all over America and for their parents and loved ones who had but to sit and wait.

The other date that will always live in my memory is June 6, 1944. I am saddened on that date each year to read some of the events of that momentous day in history. June 6, 1944 was D-Day...the day when the Allied forces stormed the beaches of Normandy.

On that day thousands of young men lost their lives doing what they were called upon to do. Planes were shot out of the sky, men in parachutes were killed while dropping behind enemy lines, boats capsized before reaching shore and men were drowned, and men were shot down on the beaches.

Many of those young men, before entering the service, had never spent a night away from home, and on that day under cover of darkness they were crossing the English Channel to face almost certain death. Some of

Troops of the 5th Engineer Special Brigad, wade through the surf to the northern coast of France, at Fox Green, Omaha Beach. They were part of the ever-increasing number of men bolstering the forces which made the initial landings on the beachhead. National Archives Photo

those kids were probably too terrified to move but had no place to go but forward.

I think most men wonder how they will react to danger when it comes. On that day those who lived found out how they would react and most found bravery and courage they could not have known was there. And those who died were just as brave or braver than many of those who lived.

Many young men, and some of my friends, made the supreme sacrifice on that day and lie in fields far from home -that is why I am always saddened on June 6th each year. Remembering can be painful too.

A DAY TO REMEMBER

Allen N. Towne provided the following which accounts for some of his memories of June 6, 1944.

The morning was gray, overcast and dismal. The visibility at first was poor, but it gradually improved. The wind was strong and the waves were about three to four feet high. The large troop transports anchored, about ten miles from shore, were rolling and some of the men were seasick

Sunrise was at about 0600 hours and low tide was about 0530 hours. H hour, the time the initial units were to hit the beach, was set at 0630 hours or about one hour after low tide.

We were awake before dawn and after a quick breakfast got ready to wait for our turn to load on to a smaller craft for the landing on Omaha beach.

I could hear the big guns on the warships firing as well as the guns on the shore. There was a great deal of smoke coming from the beach, but I could not really see what was going on.

The 18th Infantry Combat team would land in the second wave. This was scheduled for 0930. My small unit was to land on the section of OMAHA beach called Easy Red. The aid station platoon was split up into two groups so in case one group did not make it, there would be one left.

We had been waiting for over an hour, loaded with all our gear and two life preservers when we heard the L.C.I. we were supposed to go on had been sunk. We had to be rescheduled on a different landing craft. The wait was hard to take because we were all at a high pitch of excitement. It was a feeling between dread and the desire to get going and any delay increased the dread.

At last, we were told we were next to go ashore. A large tank lighter was brought alongside the Dorothea Dix. It was not normally used to carry soldiers but so many of the smaller landing craft had been sunk this was all they had.

Waiting to cross the Seine River near Melon, France. 8/27/44.

I climbed over the rail and down the side of the ship using the rope cargo net as a ladder and stepped into the bouncing landing craft. Because of the uneven pitching of the two vessels every one had to be very careful not to fall between the large ship and the smaller landing craft

Finally, we all boarded except one man who fell overboard and was caught between the two vessels. He was pulled out and did not seem to be badly hurt. He was the object of envy for he would miss the landing. We had several hundred men on the landing craft. This included a U.S. Navy shore party who were going ashore to direct Naval gunfire as well as infantrymen. Our landing boat had to circle for a while because only a few holes had been blown through the beach obstacles. We had to wait for our turn.

Off to one side, there was a barge about a half mile from the beach with four cranes sticking up like four giraffes, As I watched, a shell hit the barge on one end and it slowly started to list and sink with one side going down first. The cranes fell out into the ocean like little toys. Finally it all disappeared under the water.

As we proceeded toward shore, I could see some LCI's and smaller craft burning on the beach. As we got closer, I could see German shellfire hitting the beach. I also could see that there were many beach obstacles still in place. These beach obstacles were mined metal triangles that would rip the bottom out of the boats and then set off powerful explosives to blow up the landing craft. This meant the engineers were having trouble and we had only a few places to come ashore.

We knew that beyond the beach there would be barbed wire, concertina wire, antitank ditches, machine gun emplacements and land mines to further hinder any advance inland.

Nearby there were two destroyers, very close to shore, just drifting and firing their guns point blank at the pill boxes on the hill above the beach. The battleships were further out and were firing the big guns overhead and we could hear and feel the blast of the guns.

At last, we got clearance to land and the landing craft started in toward shore at full speed. Our group of about 20 men moved up toward the front of the landing craft.

Most of us had been on assault landings before and we wanted to be able get off before the German artillery ranged in on the tank lighter. But we did not want to be the first ones off in case there was small arms fire hitting the ramp so we positioned ourselves about five or six rows behind the lead men.

The landing craft grounded on a sand bar in about two to three feet of water. I ran down the ramp and waded to shore picking my way through the obstacles.

The German artillery shells were landing up and down the beach in a somewhat predictable manner, so we could gauge when to run and when to dive to the ground. I ran as fast as possible over the hard packed sand and went inland for about 20 feet to an area of shingle. This consisted of smooth semi-flat stones about two to three inches in diameter. The shingle led further inland to the ravine or draw we were supposed to use in exiting Omaha Beach. The stones were slippery and hard to run on. I was the senior noncom so the others followed me. I went on until I came to where about 20-30 infantry men were lying at the approach to the draw. I yelled to them to see why they were not moving out. There was no response and none of them moved. I crawled over to the nearest man to see what the problem was. I found that he was dead and so were all the others. There was a German machine gun nest at the mouth of the draw and they had all been caught in the fire as they tried to leave the beach. I immediately scuttled on my hands and legs off to the right where there was some protection from a small mound of sand. When I say scuttled I mean moving like a crab with no space between you and the ground and going fast. We had to decide what to do next.

I was seared and my mouth got so dry I could hardly talk. Sergeant Woods, who was next to me, leaned over and asked what was wrong.

I croaked back "My mouth is so dry I can't swallow never mind talk." After a short time, I calmed down and took a good look at the situation. There was no small arms fire on this section of the beach. While there were many German shells landing on the beach, they seemed to be random fire from mortars and artillery.

There were very few soldiers in the immediate area. Except for the landing boat that dropped us off, no other boat came in at this part of the beach.

Were we in the right location? We soon decided that the Navy had brought us in far to the left (east) of the proper landing spot and we had tried to leave the beach through Draw E-3. This is where the dead infantrymen were.

We were supposed to leave the beach at Draw E- 1, about a mile to our right (west). I found out later that Draw E-3 had not been secured and was still in German hands.

Our group, of about 20 men, moved west (to our right as one faced inland) all the time running and diving to the ground as the shells would come in near us.

We ran along the beach toward Draw E- I until we came to a beach aid station. Here the navy had set up a collection point where the wounded were being collected so they could be brought back aboard the ships.

At this part of Easy Red Beach, the sand portion was about 100 yards wide with areas of swamp along the inland edge of the flat. The bluff overlooking the beach was about 125 feet high and was reached by 200 yards of moderate slope, which had patches of heavy brush.

We were supposed to meet the other half of our group near here and leave the beach and go inland. First we had to find out where they were.

We used the aid station as our meeting place and while several men went looking for the other group, the rest of us went up and down the beach picking up and helping the wounded men and bringing them to the beach aid station. The beach was still under shell fire and many of the wounded men were staying in place because they did not know where to go. Others were in a partial state of shock and needed help to the aid station.

There was wreckage all along the beach. There were damaged tanks, trucks and all kinds of gear. I went by one landing craft that had dropped its ramp right in front of another exit and the Germans had opened fire as they left the boat. Many of them had been hit and killed as they tried to run down the ramp. All of the wounded had been removed, but the dead were still sprawled out in front of the vessel. The landing craft was disabled and burning half out of the water.

The beach was a shambles. I saw a tank that had come in at low tide underneath a disabled landing craft that had come in at a higher tide.

One of the unusual things I saw on the beach was a yellow Piper Cub airplane. They were used by artillery spotters. The plane seemed to be in perfect shape as if it had come over from England and landed there. About a half hour later, I saw it get hit by a shell and go up in flames

After a while, we made contact with our other aid station group and proceeded to leave the beach. We crossed the anti-tank ditch and another ditch that was flooded. We then went up the hill through the German minefield.

There was a narrow winding path through the minefield. It had been made by the first infantrymen. Some of the leading men had tripped the mines and several men, who were wounded, remained there to guide the rest of us through the mine field. They were stationed along the cleared route.

One of them had his foot blown off at the ankle. He had been bandaged up and was quite cheerful. He probably figured it was safer on the side of the hill than on the beach He knew the war was over for him. A lot of the men were envious of him.

We finally got up onto the bluff overlooking the beach. By now the 16th and 18th Infantry had infiltrated behind the Germans and had knocked out the machine gun nests and other strongpoints the Germans was using to defend Draw E-1. This portion of the beach was now secure from German small arms fire.

We dug our slit trenches and set up our temporary aid station on the beach side of the hill so the German shells would go over our heads. We started to evacuate the casualties to the beach.

From where we were, we had a good view of the beach. The engineers had cleared out several openings through the beach obstacles and were now bulldozing a road up the draw. Vehicles were starting to leave the beach area.

Enemy shells were still landing on the beach and there was a tremendous amount of wreckage on the beach. Some of the larger landing boats were still burning as more troops and vehicles were coming ashore and going inland.

The battleships and cruisers were now firing at points inland. The blast from the battleships guns could be felt where we were and we could see the incandescent shells going overhead. The targets were so far away we never heard the shells land.

Later that night, some German aircraft flew over the beachhead but there was no problem because a fleet of 4,000 vessels can throw up a lot of flak. A few German planes were shot down.

Our two groups that landed, totaling four Officers and 70 men, had seven wounded and one killed.

BEFORE WAR WAS EVER DECLARED

Al Thompson is my good friend and golfing buddy. In 1937, he was 18 years young when he enlisted in the United States Navy. His naval career spanned some 22 years. I knew Al for several years before I learned that he was even in the South Pacific. He never talked about the war and I later learned that he had spent over 50 years trying to forget some of the terrible experiences he had survived. Today, he has a hard time talking about his war years, and many of the events are all pushed together in his mind. He shared many of his memories with me because we have been close friends a long time.

In Sept. of 1939, England and France declared war on Germany. By the summer of 1940, the United States began supplying Britain with surplus war material, including aircraft. With German submarines roaming the Atlantic, the U.S. gave Britain 50 overage destroyers in exchange for the right to establish naval bases on seven British territories from Newfoundland to British Guiana.

Al was assigned to the destroyer *USS Stack* and, together with the *USS Stewart*, they escorted the aircraft carrier *Wasp* to Argentia, Newfoundland. From that location the carrier planes were able to search for German subs that were sinking ships in the convoys which carried supplies to England.

Al Thompson.

In the meantime, the British had moved 25 or 30 ships from England ports to Reykjavik, Iceland for safety. Because of the large number of German subs in the North Atlantic, it was almost impossible to get fuel and supplies to those ships boxed up in the harbor at Iceland.

The *Stack* spent many days searching for subs. They had one positive kill and another probable kill but not confirmed. The destroyer *Kearny* was damaged by a torpedo on Oct. 16, 1941 and the destroyer *Reuben James* was sunk by a torpedo on Oct. 31st, with a loss of 100 lives. Three merchant ships were also sunk. Al's ship rescued upwards of 57 survivors.

When not hunting subs, the *Stack* made several trips to Reykjavik to carry supplies to the British sailors.

These events in the North Atlantic, and many others, took place before the U. S. actually went to war with Germany and Japan.

When the Japanese struck Pearl Harbor on Dec. 7, 1941, the Wasp was ordered back to Norfolk, Va. to be escorted by the *Stack* and the *Stewart*. On the return trip, Al's destroyer was making sweeps in front of the carrier in heavy fog, always on the prowl for enemy subs. The *Stack* was rammed by the carrier and almost sunk. The crew thought they had struck a sub and kept pushing the *Stack* for several minutes. A number of men were said to have jumped overboard, thinking they were going to sink. Some perished in the fog and swirling seas. The *Stack* was heavily damaged and left with no lights and no power. The *Wasp* and the *Stewart* continued on to Norfolk, leaving the *Stack* dead in the water at the mercy of enemy subs.

The crew was terrified they would be hit by a torpedo at any moment. After about six hours, some repairs were made and the ship limped toward home, always under the threat of being torpedoed.

They were within sight of Norfolk when ordered to turn north in the bay and head for Philadelphia. As they moved into fresh water, the ship had less buoyancy and the water level rose to the ship's deck. It was necessary to send six barges to the rescue. With three barges on one side and three on the other side, cables were run beneath the destroyer and the barges practically carried the *Stack* to the shipyard. The *USS Stack* was back home for repairs and would have later exploits in the South Pacific.

Al had seen his first combat duty before the war ever started.

ON TO THE SOUTH PACIFIC

With war now officially declared, Al was able to enjoy a few months back in the states while the *USS Stack* was in the shipyard for repairs. This would be the last time for him to visit home for a long, long time. The *Stack* was about ready to embark on a journey that would take Al far from home and into many dangerous situations.

On June 5, 1942 the *Stack* joined Task Force 37, built around the Aircraft Carrier *Wasp*, and headed from Norfolk, Va. to San Diego, Calif. (History shows that the Wasp was later sunk by the Japanese.) They arrived in California on June 19th and were redesignated Task Force 18, and ordered to the South Pacific. A stop was made at Pearl Harbor on the way and Al was able to see the destruction that had occurred on Dec. 7, 1941 when the Japanese bombed Pearl Harbor.

The task force arrived Tongatapu Island on July 18th and spent five days preparing for battle before sailing for the invasion of Guadalcanal, Solomon Islands. The *Stack* covered the Guadalcanal -Tulagi landings in early August. Shortly after the Marines landed, a communiqué was issued to all of the ships in the area asking for volunteers for boat engineers and repair maintenance men on the amphibious shore craft. Al volunteered for this duty and reached his 23rd birthday a few days later on August 15, 1942. He was promised leave to go home after completing this assignment, a promise that was never fulfilled.

He spent 129 days on Guadalcanal and saw much death and destruction. Japanese submarines sank many ships through-out the area and shelled the U.S. forces on land at night. During the day Japanese planes were constantly bombing and strafing the U.S. forces. Al said that on several occasions someone standing next to him would be shot by a sniper while he was spared. At night Japanese would often infiltrate the American positions. Al survived two hand-to-hand encounters when he was attacked during the night. He remembers several times when a group of Japanese came in to surrender and one or two of them would try to throw a grenade or shoot as many U.S. soldiers as they could before they were killed themselves.

Just prior to the time Al left Guadalcanal in January of 1943 his former ship, the Stack, was ordered to return to the states for repairs. Al not only did not get his promised leave after volunteering, he missed the opportunity to go back home with the *Stack*. He was assigned to another destroyer until the *Stack* returned to the area in May. The *Stack* was assigned to Task Force 31 in July and August and was under attack by Japanese aircraft in mid July near New Georgia Island. In August, the *Stack* participated in the Battle of Vella Gulf. (This is covered in another article. History shows that the three Japanese destroyers that were sunk at Vella Gulf were the *Arashi*, the *Hagikaze* and the *Kawakaze*.)

Bougainville is the largest of the Solomon Islands and Operation Cartwheel was planned for November of 1943. The plan called for Bougainville to be invaded. It include plans to build an airfield from which they could bomb the big Japanese base at Rabaul, located 200 miles to the west on New Britain Island. Al volunteered to serve with the Marines on Bougainville. Fighting was not as fierce on Bougainville as it had been on Guadalcanal, but once again Al survived a hand-to-hand battle with a Japanese soldier. He remained on Bougainville until early December and then got leave for 10 days in Sydney, Australia. This was much needed relief for Al after serving on Guadalcanal and then on Bougainville.

USS Stack. National Archives Photo.

During the next few months Al was assigned to destroyers performing escort duty for the big task forces that were striking the Japanese in South and Central Pacific. He participated in the big attack against the large Japanese base at Truk and many other engagements against the Japanese fleet. Al dodged torpedoes many times and near misses by bombs from Japanese planes. His most vivid memories of these engagements were those times when Japanese torpedo planes would come straight at their destroyer, flying just above the water, and at the

Bernice and Allen Thompson. Married March 27, 1946. Bernice passed away on February 13, 1997.

last minute they would fly up and over the destroyer to save their torpedo for a larger U.S. warship. Of course, Al's job was below deck and it was not often that he would be able to see the action up on deck. He could hear the guns but there was no place to run down below.

In March of 1944 Al's destroyer, on escort duty, was struck by a torpedo in late evening and sunk with maybe a loss of 25 or 30 men. Al spent the night on a cork float and was picked up by another destroyer after spending 13 hours in the water. About three months later near Saipan, Al had the misfortune of being on another destroyer that was sunk by a torpedo with considerable loss of life. Al spent 17 hours in the water before being picked up by the destroyer Fletcher.

In July of 1944 Al was ordered back to the states to be reassigned. He spent the remainder of the war in California and was released on Sept. 29, 1945 as Chief Machinist Mate. He returned to the Navy in Dec. of 1945 with full rank and completed his 20 years before final discharge in November of 1959.

IN PROTECTIVE CUSTODY

While Al served on a destroyer, his younger brother served on a carrier. Their parents lived in Maryland and like other families with children in the service, his mother worried about her sons. She was a very religious lady, read her Bible every day, and practiced her religion daily. The family lived in a three level home with the bedrooms on the third floor. The parlor was on the second floor and Al's mother turned it into her bedroom after he went off to war. One night she woke up during the night and thought someone was talking to her. She thought perhaps she was dreaming but decided to go downstairs to see if what she had heard came from the lower floor. She found nothing on the lower level and returned to her bed. She was just beginning to doze when she heard a voice say, "Hester.' Hester!" She sat up in bed and said, "Make yourself known to me." She then looked in the direction from where the voice had called out to her. There on the wall was a blurred image of what Hester knew to be an angel. She was frightened. The angel spoke to her again and said, "Hester, fret no more about your boys. They are with the right hand of God and they will be protected." The angel then disappeared. Hester got out of bed and went up to the third level and woke her girls to tell them about the visit from an angel.

Al said that on a trip home his mother told him about the angel. She said she knew her boys would be safe no matter what happened and she would not worry any more.

Al was in five engagements with the Germans in the North Atlantic, and 16 engagements with the Japanese in the South Pacific. He spent over 15 hours in shark infested waters twice when ships were sunk, and survived hand-to-hand combat with the enemy on Guadalcanal. His younger brother survived 8 engagements with the Japanese.

At the time Al first heard about the angel, he was somewhat skeptical and told his mother that she must have been dreaming. In later years he would reflect on the many times he survived almost certain death and in his heart he knew the angel had been right -he had been in protective custody all during the war.

Al pitched for Carrier Baseball Team.

THIRTY-ONE KNOT BURKE

During the mid summer of 1943, in the South Pacific, U.S. forces had finally taken Guadalcanal after six months of fighting. It was learned that the Japanese were towing barges from a location about two hundred miles to the north of Guadalcanal. Al remembers the location as being called VellaVella. Under cover of darkness, submarines were apparently towing large barges, loaded with troops and supplies, and reinforcing various locations in the Solomons.

There were a large number of U.S. ships at Tulagi, across the bay from Guadalcanal, and six destroyers were ordered on a mission to destroy the barges at the point of origin. Skipper Arleigh Burke was in charge of the mission. The destination was three small islands in a triangle and four or five miles apart. One island was large enough for an airstrip, a harbor, and heavy guns mounted on shore.

Three of the destroyers were the 1650 ton class and the fastest in the navy at that time, reaching speeds of 32-33 knots. The other three destroyers had running speeds of about 31 knots. Capt. Burke had issued instructions that running speed was to be 31 knots and any destroyer unable to keep up should turn back. Their planned arrival time was midnight. One by one, three of the ships dropped out and there were only three destroyers left to complete the mission.

The crew understood the purpose of the mission was to destroy the barges but on the way they learned the mission was a bit more dangerous. The skipper informed them that they were expendable and they should say their prayers or do whatever they needed to do to put their lives in order, as they might not return from the mission.

When they arrived at their destination near midnight they pulled in close to one of the smaller islands about five miles from the main harbor. From that location their silhouettes were not visible but they could see the main harbor on the larger island. It was then that the crew realized the real purpose of their mission. Across the harbor they were able to see a heavy cruiser, two troop transports (estimated 10,000 men on each ship), three destroyers, and possibly some

Left, Capt. A.A. Burke, USN and Capt. T.J. Hedding, USN right, aboard USS Lexington (CV 16) during attack on Saipan in the Marianas. National Archives Photo.

submarines to one side. These ships had apparently just arrived in harbor and they could be heard moving around and dropping anchor.

The men on board the destroyers, sitting there in the darkness, were ready but terrified they would be spotted. Those were anxious moments while waiting for the right moment to strike.

Each of the three destroyers had 8 torpedoes on each side, or a total of 48 torpedoes in all. The destroyers moved out in the harbor from their hiding place and fired their torpedoes from one side, then circled and fired those from the other side. In 22 minutes they had sunk the heavy cruiser, the two troop ships, and three destroyers. Al said they could see thousands of men in the water as the ships went down. The heavy guns on shore opened fire into the air, apparently thinking bombs were from planes overhead.

The three destroyers headed back to base as fast as they could get out of there. At break of day they were attacked by about 16 Japanese planes. Two bombs came close to the *Stack* but there were no hits. U.S. planes intercepted the Japanese planes and Al could see them in dogfights up above. The destroyers arrived back in Talagi about 7AM, and there were no casualties on any of the ships.

Capt. Burke made Rear Admiral after that mission, and received the nickname "31 knot Burke". Arleigh Burke has been remembered as a gung-ho leader that navy personnel would have followed any place. He was later made Chief of Naval Operations.

A SPECIAL CALL TO HOME

My good friend Carl Courtney was raised in West Virginia. He enlisted in the U. S. Navy at age 19 on June 14, 1943 in Parkersburg, W. Va. He was sent to boot camp at Great Lakes, Ill. From there he was sent to Norfolk, Va. to a DE (destroyer escort) school. From there he was sent to Charleston, S.C. where they were building a number of destroyer escorts. Carl was assigned to the USS Neuendorf, DE-200. Carl Courtney remained in the U. S. Navy for 30 years and retired in 1973. He rose up through the ranks to become a Lt. Commander.

War was raging in Europe and in the South Pacific - the year was 1943. The skipper of the *USS Neuendorf* had watched his ship being built at the Charleston, S. C. ship yard. He had assembled his crew and they had watched every nut and bolt that went into the ship. They knew where every circuit and every steam line ran. The officer and his crew became like family. The ship was completed in the fall of 1943 and put out to sea for a trial run so the crew could practice the things they had learned and how to respond to every emergency. They were even able to handle a real emergency when they located and sank a German submarine. They had learned their jobs well and returned to Charleston.

It was now December and the skipper wanted to reward his crew for their performance by giving them leave before it was time to head for the South Pacific. After all, Christmas was just a few weeks away and it would be nice for his crew to visit home and bid goodbye to their families before heading into harm's way.

The skipper allowed half of the crew to go on leave and the other half of the crew remained on board the ship in Charleston Harbor. The first group was due back on board ship on December 17th. Carl Courtney, a young engineer on the ship, decided he would stay on the ship as there was much to do while others were away.

Since half of the crew would be back on the morning of December 17th, the skipper decided to let the other half of the crew catch the evening train on the night of the 16th, which meant there would be a few hours when all of the crew would be gone. A winter storm had moved into the Carolinas that night and it was snowing when a large number of the crew boarded the northbound Atlantic Coast Line passenger train out of Charleston.

The southbound ACL passenger train was due to arrive Charleston during the early morning hours of the 17th. At 1:15AM, 12 miles north of Lumberton, N. C., the southbound train derailed due to a broken rail. Several of the derailed cars tilted over on the northbound track. Some of the train crew, knowing that the northbound train would be arriving in about 15 minutes, moved down the track in front of the derailed train to try and flag down the northbound train. Due to the blinding snow, the engineer did not see the men waving their lanterns, and the northbound train Slammed into the derailed cars of the southbound train. It was a catastrophe.

The New York Times on Dec. 17, 1943 reported that between 60 and 100 were killed and more than 100 injured. The majority of those killed and wounded were servicemen. The crew of the *USS Neuendorf* was over sixty percent wiped out in the wreckage of those two trains. Most of those homeward bound for Christmas never made it.

Carl had loaned his winter navy jacket to one of the sailors headed home for Christmas. Inside that jacket Carl had inscribed his name. When the initial list of casualties was posted, Carl's name was on the list. He immediately called home to let his mother know that he was alive. He was not a casualty of the train wreck.

USS NEUENDORF

After Christmas of 1943 the *USS Neuendorf* set sail for the South Pacific with a new crew that had to be trained. This meant new responsibilities for Carl. Before heading for the Panama Canal a stopover was made in New Orleans. In January of 1944, the DE-200 set sail with four other destroyer escorts, the DE-198, DE-199, DE-201, and the DE-202. After a stop in Bora-Bora for refueling, the group headed for New Caledonia. They arrived in New Caledonia on Jan. 28, 1944.

They first met up with a large task force heading north, probably in search of the Japanese fleet and to inflict damage on Japanese land positions on the way. Carl said he thought this was Task Force No. 53. The destroyer escorts were assigned to escort the support ships such as tankers, ammunition ships, supply ships, etc. This group of ships would supply the task force and then meet with them again when they returned for fuel and supplies.

During February and March the escorts worked with some of the forces making strikes in the Gilbert Islands and the Solomon Islands. Now and then they were allowed to go on shore in the New Hebrides Islands where they could relax on the sand and drink beer.

The *USS Neuendorf* was assigned to General McArthur's forces in April and for the next four months they worked with landings being made along the east coast of New Guinea. The *USS Neuendorf* would frequently be called on to search a harbor for submarines before a mine sweeper went in to check for mines. Landings would be made, the area secured, and then the larger group would move on to the next location. On April 23rd strong forces were landed on Hollandia, New Guinea with naval support. Carl had never seen so many ships in one place. Biak Island to the north of New Guinea was invaded on May 27th. After Biak was secured the DE-200 returned to working with supply ships for the large task forces striking Japanese positions further to the north.

There were cannibals in some parts of New Guinea but mostly the natives were very friendly. When at anchor off shore, a security guard was always on duty to prevent anyone from coming on board the ship. On one occasion a native came out to the ship and was able to speak a little English. He said there was a plane down a short distance from the shore. Investigation developed there were no survivors.

The crew from the DE-200 was allowed to go on shore at one location in New Guinea and the male natives lined up on the shore. The women lined up a short distance back in the edge of the forest. The chaplain noticed that the women had no covering above the waist. He returned to the ship and returned with T-shirts for the females. The women eagerly put on their new attire but promptly cut holes in the shirts to allow room for their breasts to stick through.

Carl said all of the children were naked and appeared to be about the same size. Each of the kids had a spear and they were easily spearing fish in the water. Each youngster had a string of fish over the shoulder. When the sailors tried to spear the fish they came up empty and the natives would just laugh at their efforts. The men all had machetes and were very skillful in slicing thin pieces from the coconut trees. Some of the larger sailors thought they could do better than the natives but they were not able to handle the machetes like the natives.

Amid all of the horrors of war, the sailors were able to enjoy their brief stay on shore. There, for a short time, the crew of the *Neuendorf* met with a people who held no hatred for anyone. They knew how to laugh and respond to friendship.

ON TO THE PHILIPPINES

On March 29, 1944 a strong task force struck Palau Islands. Enemy planes spotted the task force and the Japanese ships fled the area. Later, on September 14th, the marines swarmed on Peleliu, one of the southern islands in the Palau group. Upon reaching the beaches the marines were met by determined ground forces and fierce artillery and mortar fire. Records show that the marines pushed ahead rapidly. When the *USS Neuendorf* arrived at Peleliu there were literally hundreds of bodies in the water, both marines of the First Division and the Japanese. Losses were obviously extremely heavy in the initial landing.

On October 20th the Philippines were invaded at Leyte. While forces struggled on land, battle raged in Leyte Gulf and the Philippine Sea during October 23-26. The Japanese lost 58 warships sunk or damaged, including four carriers and two battleships. The United States lost the light carrier Princeton, two escort carriers, two destroyers, and one destroyer escort. The *USS Neuendorf* helped pick up survivors in Leyte Gulf. Carl boarded one of the destroyers before it went down to try and get a lathe from their machine shop. He was unable to get the lathe before he had to leave. He looked down the hatch while on board and could see men who had been scalded to death while trying to escape up the ladder. The destroyer went down a short time after Carl left the ship.

It took two months to defeat the Japanese on Leyte, with 11,217 American casualties and 113,231 Japanese casualties. Carl said the Japanese suicide planes came out in full force.

The largest ship that Carl saw sinking (a tanker) was near Mindoro in the southern Philippines. The tanker was loaded with aviation fuel. As they approached, the tanker was attacked by two Japanese planes. The tanker was hit and exploded in a ball of flames and black smoke. By the time the *USS*

Neuendorf reached the scene the ship was completely gone, and nothing was left except a few life jackets floating on the surface and a piece of cord where the tanker had been tied up.

The *USS Neuendorf* went through Surigao Strait to the west side of the Philippines. They were on general quarters all the time around the Philippines and through the Strait. There were constant air attacks and the threat of land based torpedoes in the Strait. When they arrived in the South China Sea there were ships burning and sticking up out of the water everywhere. The Japanese ships had been the target of many air attacks by U. S. pilots.

While the *Neuendorf* was taking on fuel next to a tanker, a Japanese plane approached and was shot down, landing in the water near by. The pilot fell out of the plane as it approached the water and landed on the gun turret on the tanker, the *USS Kankakee*. The dead pilot had a map in his pocket showing where that particular group of ships was supposed to be each hour of that day.

The *Neuendorf* participated in the landings at Lingayen Gulf in January of 1945, 100 miles north of Manila.

Carl said while they were on the west side of the Philippines at Iloilo as he watched the contents of a cargo ship being unloaded into a truck. As the truck left the dock and headed down the road, he saw the locals block the road with an ox, steal the load from the truck and head off in the forest.

Okinawa was invaded oil April 1st and fighting continued there until June 21st. The *Neuendorf* participated in part of that operation. They were attacked by a Kamikaze suicide plane on one occasion. The plane came in over the top of the ship's torpedo launcher, crashed into the sea next to the ship and left his tail section hung up on the hand rail of the ship. What a close call.'

While in the Okinawa area, a typhoon struck and five destroyers were sunk. The little destroyer escort rode out the storm and also helped rescue some of the survivors.

After the atomic bombs were dropped on Japan, the *USS Neuendorf* returned to San Diego on October 25, 1945. She had been on tour in the South Pacific 21 months and 23 days. Carl was a First Class Machinist Mate. The ship had traveled 102,816 miles - maximum speed about 20 knots.

A COURAGEOUS YOUNG MAN

In time of war, many courageous young men rush to the defense of their country. They often give little thought to what they will be doing or whether they will be suited for a specific assignment. They are anxious to serve, to challenge themselves and prove they can handle the toughest assignments. Perhaps that was the case for my friend Jams Logan, and for me and many others.

Jim first tried the Naval Air Force which was very difficult to get into. Qualifying tests and an all day physical weeded out those with imperfections. Jim made it through the qualifying rounds and was sent to LeHigh University for college courses as well as flying lessons. This training was to last for about three months. In the early days of this Navy program, the men had no uniforms and received no pay. It was a tough assignment, with long hours of study before dawn and into the night and learning to fly a strange machine called an airplane during daylight hours. Jim got past the solo stage of flight training and then ran into a tough inspector on a check flight and was turned down for further flight training. He had "washed out".

Jim was born in Philadelphia, Pennsylvania. He then enlisted in the U.S. Army in September of 1942. He was a tough kid, not to be outdone, so he volunteered for Paratroop Training and was sent to Toccoa, Ga. In two months, he came down with almost endless coughing and high fever. He was hospitalized for a month. Another wash-out. He was then assigned to the 131st Infantry Regiment and sent with 200 other washouts to Sault Ste. Marie, Michigan to guard the shipping locks along the Canadian border. From there he was sent to Camp Van Dorn, Miss. for a few weeks of infantry training. Next stop was Ft. Benning, Ga. Then, he and 300 other non-coms were sent to Camp Atterbury, Indiana to fill slots in the 30th Division. The Division shipped out to Boston, Mass. and boarded a converted luxury liner, *U.S.S.*

Argentina, and sailed to England in Feb. of 1944. The convoy was comprised of over 100 ships, including two massive aircraft carriers. Jim was assigned to B Company, 120th Infantry, 30th Division.

The Division landed at Firth of Clyde, Scotland and moved by train to Bognor Regis, Sussex, England. They were billeted in private homes. Invasion news was the topic of the day during the weeks that followed. General Eisenhower had told them they wouldn't be in the first wave, but they wouldn't be in the last, either. Jim wrote of the invasion as follows in one of his newspaper articles:

James O. Logan.

"What was called 'The Greatest Show on Earth' had already happened. The Americans, the British, the Canadians, all were now on the beaches of Normandy. And B Company tried to get some sleep as the nondescript gray ship chugged up and down the English Channel to kill time until a rendezvous could be made with similar vessels carrying other Americans.

By the time we caught our first glimpse of the Normandy beaches, it was D plus two. It was June 8th. We had been trying to get some sleep on a British ship without a bed or bunk of any description. We slept on our feet, on our packs, on the decks, and on each other. By the time we climbed down the cargo net into the pitching landing craft, there wasn't a pair of eyes among us which were not bloodshot.

The trip to the beach took 20 minutes or so. Those flat-bottomed craft were designed to be as buoyant as possible. And this one lived up to that standard. There must have been 50 infantrymen on board. Because this craft was so buoyant, we assumed it would drop us off rather close to dry land. We heard the sound metal boats make when they scrape bottom. The Englishman in army uniform whose job it was to take a group of 50 to the shore, and then go back to the ship for another 50, pulled a lever and the front wall of the stilled boat parted from its moorings and splashed into the salty water. From that point it was at least 100 yards from dry land.

Everyone had the same idea: Take a few fast steps and plunge, feet first, into the water. It would probably be deep enough to come to our hips. We wondered how cold it would be. After being in the bright sunlight, the water seemed unmercifully cold. Worse than that, though, was the depth of the water. It came to my armpits. The bandoleers of ammunition, the cartridge belts, the rifle and helmet, all these gave us stability. The field pack gave us buoyancy. My six-foot height kept my head well above water. Something bumped into me below the surface. It clawed its way upward. It was another member of the company. He was too short for this sort of thing. We pulled off his helmet and let it sink. We stripped him of three rounds of 37 mm mortar shells and carried them ashore. A tall Texan walked to the beach, carrying our short comrade. He had come close to being the first casualty.

We walked inland and saw our first dead, Americans and Germans. It was our first encounter with the reality of war. Seeing men in American uniforms, covered with blood, was something we expected but could not imagine until now. There were dead Germans as well. Someone said something about the fallen super race. That night we talked about it. We had never before seen German soldiers. We marveled at their handsome features, their blond hair. One of our snipers remarked that he would find it difficult to kill someone who looked like he should be on a college campus, or in a Broadway play.

That night each squad was to post a guard. We didn't. We felt it might be the last night we would get any worthwhile sleep. When we awoke, we discovered that one of our sergeants had shot himself in the foot. It was hard to believe. Everyone was noticeably nervous because of what was to come. But the very idea of deliberately crippling oneself, after all the preparations and training, made no sense at all.

We moved ahead. We found German soldiers who were as frightened as we were. Perhaps a little more so because they were surrendering. None of us had yet fired a shot. But the realities of war soon became known. Machine guns chattered at us continuously. Why more of us were not wounded or killed, I am not sure. Perhaps we were being fired on from too great a distance.

For the first 14 days, no one shaved. No one bathed. We slept when we stopped moving. And sometimes it seemed we didn't stop for days at a time. We were pulled off the line after two weeks and marched three or four miles to the rear where a portable shower tent had been set up. We showered with hot water and Ivory Soap. We put on clean clothes."

For more than a week the town of St. Lo blocked the advance of American troops on the western end of the Normandy battle front. A hard battle was fought to take St. Lo before it was taken by the Americans on July 18, 1944. On July 17th, during the battle for St. Lo, Jim was hit by a shell fragment which smashed his humerus at the right elbow. Another fragment from the same shell ripped through his left thigh. He could not walk and, in desperate pain, he remained where he was for 18 hours. His closest friend, Douglas Thomas, insisted on staying with him until he was picked up in a jeep.

Jim was taken to a Battalion Aid Station. From there he was moved to the evacuation hospital, a huge almost circus-size tent, humming with activity, occasional moans and the smell of rotting flesh. Jim was put on a stretchercarrier and wheeled a hundred yards over a piece of farmland to a waiting twin engine aircraft. He was taken to a U.S.A. hospital in Wales where he remained for two months. He was later moved to Deshon Amy Hospital in Butler, Pa. where he remained for nine months. He was finally moved to Camp Pickett, Va. for rehab for two months and discharged in September of 1946. James Logan was a corporal.

Jim reflected on his days in France when he wrote: "War brings men closer together. My life was saved 20 or 30 times because someone fired at the enemy when I couldn't see him. That meant someone had to give away his position.

When the war ended, we went home. Today, I couldn't remember the names of a dozen men who fought in that same infantry company on that far-away peninsula. We were frightened silly. All of us. And we took turns being brave. But, then, maybe all wars are like that."

Courageous young men like Jim have always stepped forward to put their lives on the line when the need was there. That is why we enjoy our freedom today. My hat is off to each one of them.

HE FAILED TO SALUTE

After James Logan was seriously wounded in France, he laid in a field near St. Lo for 18 hours before being picked up by a jeep. Jim wrote to me about an incident which happened as he was receiving first aid.

"I was taken to a battalion aid station where I found my friend, Chaplain Gunter Tileman (Captain). Lord knows when he had any sleep, and looked it. He spoke some comforting words and then had to run to assist the doctor with plasma. Then, on to the evac hospital, a huge almost circus-size tent, humming with activity, occasional moans and the smell of rotting flesh.

I stopped an orderly to tell him I had an additional emergency, aside from my wounds. I had to GO! I was hoping he would help me to a latrine, but he returned with a shiny, new bed pan, leaving it with me.

James Logan, taken May 1944. London.

There must have been more than a hundred men on cots in that tent. I was determined to give that impersonal bed pan a try, but my right arm was useless. The left thigh, although not too serious, had a shell fragment tunnel running through that big, upper-thigh muscle without having touched the bone. Nevertheless, I couldn't use it to help me get on that damned bed pan!

The cots in the tent had less than a foot of space between them. The man on my right said, "C'mon, Buddy, I can sit up, here, and help you." The man on my left, also appreciating my problem, volunteered to help. I appreciated their sincerity, but, at that time, wanted more to crawl under the tent flap and run, not walk, to rejoin my outfit. Under such conditions, that would have been impossible.

So, the man on the right, with both legs broken from a mine, sat up and with great effort - the sweat was pouring down his face -undid my belt while I sat up, balancing myself with the left hand and arm. The man on the left, seeing the valiant effort on the part of myself and the soldier to my right, also joined in. The orderlies were so busy they never saw this crazy comedy of errors.

In what seemed an age, my undershorts were cut off with a trenchknife, still in the possession of the benefactor to my left.

Three men never worked harder under such painful circumstances.

Then, with my right am in a bandage-sling, applied at the Battalion Aid Station, I became the only soldier in that mass of pain and suffering who was sitting upright - on that impersonal bed pan.

At least I knew my distorted stomach was about to be relieved. I was sure, in spite of the embarrassing situation, everyone in a cot, who could, was watching me. Relief was just a breath away.

No such luck. I was pronounced "dehydrated" by the orderly, who took a precious moment to remove the pan, get my torn and tattered uniform pants back in place and announced that I would soon be on a plane to Britain, where the matter could more easily be handled.

My 'helpers' - both the left and right one, as well as myself, couldn't hold back our laughter. I told them both there should be a special medal for the assistance they so willingly gave. It was only then that this enlisted man noticed the soldier on the left was a captain. The one on the right was a major. I told them I had missed a golden opportunity to salute both of them while I was mounted on the bed pan."

"WAR IS HELL"

Edward J. Cooper, Jr. graduated from Maury High School in Norfolk, Va. in June of 1942 and entered V.P.I. in Blacksburg, Va. Because of the war, most educational institutions had begun an accelerated program of study. However, by March of 1943 95% of the student body had either entered or was preparing to enter the armed forces.

Eddie, along with many of his friends, took a test to qualify for the Navy V-12 program. After waiting a reasonable time for a reply, and thinking he had not been accepted, Eddie went to the Draft Board and asked to be drafted. An

Edward J. Cooper. Summer of 1944.

acceptance letter from the Navy had been delivered to the wrong address and was finally delivered to his mother the day Eddie reported for duty in the army at Fort Lee, Va. A delayed letter from the Navy altered -Eddie's military career - he was now in the United States Amy.

Eddie was sent to Aberdeen MD. for basic training in the Ordinance Corps. In August he was selected for the Army Specialized Training Corps (ASTP) a program designed to enable those qualified to complete college and be sent to Officers Candidate School (OCS). Much to Eddie's surprise, he ended up in ASTP back at V.P.I. in Blacksburg, Va. He remained there until March of 1944. At that time, a troop train pulled into Blacksburg to transport the entire army student body to an unknown destination. According to Eddie, there were 3,000 "Sad Sacks" on that train. This group of young men from V.P.I. and other ASTP units ended up at Camp Claiborne, La. and were assigned to the 84th Infantry Division as Privates. The Division was already staffed with noncommissioned and commissioned officers. Infantry basic training there lasted from April through August of 1944. In September the Division was boarded on troop trains and sent to Camp Kilmer, NJ, ready for overseas duty. On Sept. 20, 1944 Eddie's battalion boarded the *SS Thomas Barry* for a rough 10-day voyage in a convoy to Southhampton, England.

Company L, of the 334th Infantry Regiment of the 84th Infantry Division, Eddie's unit, was billeted in the small village of Alresford, England, for the entire month of October.

Eddie was fortunate to get a two-day pass to London. The excitement of seeing many historic landmarks he had read about was tempered by seeing the devastation caused by the German bombing. However, his fondest memories of Jolly Ole England revolved around a wonderful family, Maude and Philip Hartland and daughter Nghare. Eddie and three of his close buddies met Mrs. Hartland and Nghare at a small service club in Alresford and were invited for "tea" the next day. It was uncanny how all became such good friends and the frequent visits became a welcomed respite from army life. Riding horseback over the scenic countryside with Nghare was an unforgettable experience. Despite later happenings, Eddie remained in touch with the family, even visiting them many times after the war. Nghare and her English husband have even vacationed with Eddie and his wife in Virginia. (Eddie was the sole survivor of the foursome that frequented the Hartland home.)

The 84th Infantry Division left England on Halloween night, October 31,1944. They crossed the English Channel and landed at Omaha Beach, one of the main beaches invaded on D-Day of June 6, 1944. Eddie was amazed at all of the wreckage left behind from the terrible ordeal of the earlier landings on that beach. There was evidence of the horrible destruction that had taken place at that location where so many lives had been lost.

Eddie walked nine miles in new foot-blistering boots, through the rain and mud, and was completely exhausted when time came to set up camp. He was immediately instructed to dig a latrine. He had just completed that assignment when an officer came along and said "now you can dig one for the officers." I need not tell you the thoughts that went through Eddie's mind at that very moment. I'm sure he could have been court martialed if one could be convicted on thoughts and not words.

The group remained at this location for six days and thew they were loaded on trucks and moved through St. Lo, on through Paris, and headed north. They camped two different nights on this trip and it was wet and rainy and miserable. They went through the southern tip of Belgium into Holland and stopped in a small village near the city of Masstricht. The farm where they encamped had two large barns facing each other and a large brick home was at one end - it was sort of a U shape arrangement. The soldiers were billeted in the bay loft of the barns.

Eddie was to witness the birth of a calf during the one week they were there. Being a city boy, it was an exciting experience for him. At this location, the soldiers would cut bars of soap into several pieces and trade them for beer. Eddie still remembers the wonderful pancakes prepared by the mess wagon just before moving up to the front lines. They were served with heated syrup and butter. Eddie said, "its funny the things we remember"!

There was an organ in the reception hall of the farmhouse and the family occasionally would gather around and sing Dutch songs and Christmas carols, which of course were sung in Dutch. The soldiers would listen to the songs and join in by singing the words in English when possible. It was November 17th, Christmas was approaching, and the soldiers were far from home.

Just before moving up to the front, mail call was received and only a few letters arrived, one of which was addressed to Eddie. Eddie opened the perfumed letter , sealed with a kiss, and it was from a girl friend with whom he had been rather close. Unfortunately, the letter was addressed, inside, to another man, and told about how much she had enjoyed the weekend, etc. The letter intended for Eddie no doubt went to the other man. What an accidental switch! The soldiers moved toward the outskirts of Geilenkirchen, Germany. Along the way they met a few German prisoners who were smiling and chatting, in German, with the American troops. Eddie could not help but remember thinking how they looked just like he did and what in the world were they doing trying to kill each other. Of course, he well understood the Nazi cause and why they were there.

Before moving on to the front, they were told to carry all the food they could carry as it might not be possible to get food up to them. Eddie and others stuffed their shirts with all the rations they could cram in. When the Germans started shelling, Eddie said everyone hit the dirt until they felt it was safe to proceed. They quickly discovered that all those rations packed in their shirts and pockets made them better targets. Eddie said, "When under fire, you want to hug mother earth like a snake and the food interfered, so out went the rations". A lot of food had to be discarded. Along the way there were dead cows and horses and the stench was terrible.

They arrived at the front in the dark on November 18th They dug their fox holes as quickly as possible while shells were coming in. One of Eddie's buddies called out to him that he wasn't going to make it and asked that he notify his wife that he loved her. The young man was later killed so he must have had a premonition of death.

Eddie's group had been loaned to the British 2nd Army and they were near the northern end of the Siegfried line. The troops remained at this location for five days and up ahead they could see the German pill boxes. Several British tanks approached the pill boxes and were immediately knocked out by the German guns. The tanks were burning, ammunition was exploding, and men came tumbling out of the tanks with clothing on fire. It was a horrible sight but nothing could be done. On

Eddie Cooper at the Miss America Pagent in Atlantic City, NJ. September 1945.

November 23rd the troops started moving forward under the cover of darkness. Eddie hit the ground as shell fire came in fast and furiously. All of a sudden, he felt a burning sensation in his upper left thigh and then felt the warmth of the blood in his trousers. He couldn't move and was going into shock, when he called out that he had been hit. Somehow, someone got to him and applied a tourniquet as his femoral artery had been severed. He could remember hearing others yelling also as he passed out. He lost track of time but came to, strapped on a stretcher on a jeep, and next to him was Sgt. Montleon. The sergeant died on the way back to the battalion aid station. In the company of 120 men, 20 were killed that night. A number of Americans were taken prisoners, including the company commander, and many were wounded.

Eddie was taken back to the hospital , a former monastery, in Masstricht, and given lots of plasma which probably saved his life. Many deaths occurred in the hospital in Holland. Eddie had a long, jagged wound in his thigh and because the blood supply had been shut off to the lower leg, Eddie was unable to feel pins when stuck in his foot. Gangrene had set in. It was necessary to remove his foot at the ankle on December 1st.

On December 5th, he was sent to England to the 103rd General Hospital in Tidworth. Most patients went into a ward but Eddie, who had taken a turn for the worse, was not expected to survive, so he was placed in a private room. However, he made it and was moved to a ward in about a week. Eddie remained in England from December 5th until late February of 1945. It was necessary for Eddie to have several more operations as he lost more of his leg and eventually the leg was removed to about two and one half inches below the knee.

The Red Cross got in touch with the English family that had befriended Eddie during the month of October. The first day Eddie was allowed to be on crutches, his English friends showed up in front of the hospital in a big car, with warmers and blankets in the back seat. They had pre-arranged this with the hospital . Eddie was taken to their home for 30 hours. He received tender loving care from these wonderful friends he had known only a short time.

Eddie was then moved to Bristol, England where he remained for two weeks. He was then flown to Glasgow, Scotland where he remained for two days. Then he left for the USA on a hospital plane with a stop in the Azores for fuel, a two day stop in Newfoundland due to a blizzard, then on to Mitchell Field in Long Island, N. Y. From there he was flown to Atlantic City where a

Field in Long Island, N. Y. From there he was flown to Atlantic City where a large hotel, the Haddon Hall-Chalfunt, had been turned into a hospital. This was now March 2, 1945. Eddie continued to have additional operations on his leg, the final one in the summer of 1945.

Eddie said there were 3000 amputees at this location and they were frequently entertained by shows and show people from New York. The Red Cross and Army Special Services did a super job of providing entertainment. They attended football games at Franklin Field in Philadelphia, concerts at the Academy of Music, and big USO shows at a large auditorium in Philadelphia.

When VE Day arrived, the amputees who could not get out, tore open their pillows and threw the feathers and makeshift balloons out the windows of the high-rise hospital. Jubilation was rampant. Kisses and hugs, screaming and shouting like New Years Eve, only more so.

Eddie was fitted with several legs and continued to have problems until May of 1946. The Atlantic City facility was closed down in April of 1946 and he was sent to Walter Reed Hospital for three months and was released on July 20, 1946.

THE NIGHT FIGHTER

Jack Tefft was one of those young men who was subject to the draft in the months prior to the Japanese attack on Pearl harbor. Jack was born in Pennsylvania and, to avoid the draft, he enlisted in the Navy aviation cadet program. He was called to active duty in September of 1941 and reported to Philadelphia, Pa. Jack called this phase of training the "Elimination Base." After completion of this training Jack was sent to Jacksonville, Fla. for primary, secondary, and advanced flight training. He graduated in June of 1942 and received his wings as an Ensign.

Jack was then sent to Washington, D. C. to tile Anacosta Naval Air Station and from there to the new Naval Air Test Center at Patuxent, River, Maryland. He remained there from the summer of 1943 until January 1944.

He volunteered for night fighters in the F6F Hellcat. He was sent to a squadron in Rhode Island where they trained for five months and then flew to California and boarded a converted carrier, destination Hawaii. There, they trained for a couple of months and boarded the aircraft carrier *USS Enterprise* with Air Group 20. The *Enterprise* headed for the combat area.

He recalled one occasion when he was on Combat Air Patrol (CAP) over the American task force and he saw the *USS Princeton* when it was struck by a Japanese suicide plane called a Kamikaze. (The *USS Princeton* was actually sunk during the battle of Leyte Gulf Oct. 23-26, 1944)

All together, Jack lost close to one third of his squadron. Most losses stemmed from anti aircraft fire or enemy aircraft. Often, planes would go off on a mission and never return. The fate of the pilot would remain a mystery.

Jack made 120 carrier landings and 49 night landings while in combat during the war. He said night intercepts of enemy aircraft were made by radar but the enemy was not around much at night during that period. Therefore, most of their activities were during the day.

who was compiling some stories about the squadron:

"I have been very reluctant in recent years to put any '&sea stories' in writing, primarily because my stories reflect the aging trend of: The older I get, the Better I was. But since this story doesn't claim any heroics on my part, here goes:

We were flying off Enterprise and I was part of the fighter cover for the bomber and torpedo planes. The strike was against shipping in Manila Bay and I believe CAG "Dog" Smith was the leader. The overcast was heavy and low so we reached the target by flying South around the island rather than directly over the cloud covered mountains to Manila. This of course took much time and fuel, so when we reached the target area "Dog" directed that we make a one run attack on the ships and then expedite to rendezvous point at Cavite. Fighter planes carried rockets and in our attack mine did not fire. I had forgotten to turn on my master arm switch. On the way to the rendezvous point I saw a medium sized vessel leaving the harbor so I signaled my wing man, Beveridge, that I was going to fire my rockets at it, which I did. When I pulled out of the run none of my flight was in sight, including Beveridge. About that time I saw an aircraft in the distance heading in the opposite direction with it's wheels down. I thought it was a TBF in trouble so I proceeded to join on him. As I got closer I could see that it was Japanese and had a long canopy. I immediately charged my guns and on the first burst it started flaming and two people were crawling out on the wing as it completely burned and went in. It was later identified as a "Sonia", an old fixed landing gear aircraft.

At this point I was heading away from the rendezvous point and close to the city of Manila, so I flow up into the overcast, climbing to safe altitude above the mountains on course toward our Task Force. When I reported in to Enterprise they directed me to "conserve fuel" and since I was a night fighter I would be recovered last. The sun was now setting and the ship was steaming toward the flight that was at least an hour away and running low on fuel.

As we all remember, that was the night that many aircraft ditched and there were many exciting stories about getting aboard.

Enterprise eventually sent me over to land aboard Franklin which I did after they cleared away a TBF barrier crash.

I did not get back to Enterprise until the next day; about noon. Most everyone was surprised to see me. Because in all the confusion, the Ready

Jack Tefft.

Room had not been notified that I had landed aboard Franklin and they thought I was among the missing. In fact some of my friends were dividing up my little bottles of brandy."

Jack also served for a short time on the Aircraft Carrier *USS Lexington*. In February of 1945, Jack returned to the states and was sent to Atlantic City to reform with Fighting Squadron 20. From there he met the rest of the air group in Edenton, N. C. The war ended and Jack remained in the Navy as a career regular Naval Officer.

After the war ended, Jack was selected for a touring air show called the "Navy's Flying Might". It was set up by the Treasury Dept. to sell "Victory Bonds". The group performed in 35 cities from the East coast to the West coast and back during the fall of 1945. Jack was part of a Corsair aerobatic team.

Jack rose to the rank of Captain and retired from the Navy in September of 1972 after 31 years of service to his country.

John Blair enlisted in the U. S. Navy in Charleston, S.C. at age 18 in

THE YEOMAN

John Blair enlisted in the U. S. Navy in Charleston, S.C. at age 18 in April of 1943. John and I are in the same golf group but it was a long time before I learned that we both had grown up in the same town in Tennessee.

John was sent to Boot Camp in Bainbridge, Md. for nine weeks. From there he was sent to Norfolk, Va. to the Dam Neck facility where he learned to use the 90 millimeter anti-tank, anti-aircraft gun.

In September of 1943, he was sent to Mare Island in California in preparation for the South Pacific. After a short stay there he was moved to Tiburon, near San Francisco, for floating dry dock and seaman training. He was later sent to Morgan City, La. where the *USS ABSD-5* (advance base sectional dock) was being built.

The seven sections of this dry dock were towed through the Panama Canal. Some sections were so large they would not clear the canal and it was necessary for the Seabees, under the command of the Naval Civil Engineer Corps, to tip the mammoth dock on its side to pull it through the canal. They arrived at Guiuan Harbor off the coast of Samar in the Philippine Islands in Feb. 1945. Each of the seven sections of the dry dock was a complete ship except they were not self propelled. Dry docks such as these were moved as close to the combat zone as possible in order to get ships repaired and back in service as quickly as possible.

The largest ship this dry dock was supposed to handle was the cruiser class but, with some difficulty, they managed to handle the battleships *Mississippi* and *Idaho*. The *USS Mississippi* had been hit by a Japanese suicide plane. This dry dock repaired a great many landing craft and troop ships, including the *USS Audubon* and *Lubbock*. They also repaired the *USS Wildcat*, a water distilling ship. The Norwegian ship *SS Kirkenes* was repaired at the dry dock and John remembers the many pretty girls that were part of

USS Mississippi coming into dock.

Dry Dock.

the crew. A total of 54 ships were repaired at this facility, the last of which was the troop ship *USS Selinur* in Dec. of 1945.

John was a Yeoman during his early days in the Navy, and received his discharge in April of 1946 in San Francisco. He was in and out of the Navy two other times before retiring in 1968 with 20 years service. He was a Senior Chief DP (Data Processing).

Senior Chief Data Processing Tech. John Blair and wife Thelma.

THE FLIGHT INSTRUCTOR

We always call him Romie but his real name is Roman Stutzman. Romie was born in Ohio but raised in Norfolk, Va. He will be 85 years old come May of 1997.

When the United States entered the war in December of 1941, Romie already owned his own airplane. At age 30, he was too old to become an aviation cadet. When the War Dept. issued a call for civilian pilots to serve as instructors, he reported to Richmond, Va. and was sworn in the Reserve as a private. While he carried the rank of private, he was officially carried on the Civil Service payroll with pay equal to that of an officer.

Roman Stutzman.

Romie returned to Norfolk where the local civilian flying school was being closed to accommodate a class of P-40 fighter pilots being assigned to the airport for training. The local group moved to Lawrenceville, Va. and started a Civilian Pilot Training (CPT) school to develop pilot instructors. This would be Romie's first assignment as an instructor. They flew Piper Cubs and Wacos.

Romie was later sent to Maxwell Field in Montgomery, Ala. to fly PT-17's and learn to teach the army way. From there he went to Kelly Field in

San Antonio, Tex. where he trained in the PT-19. From there he was sent to Garner Field in Tex. where he taught aviation cadets in primary flight training.

The Air Corps finally began to get their quota of pilots and needed fewer instructors. Romie was sent to Randolph Field near San Antonio to learn instrument flying in the BT-13. From there, he was sent to Houston for multi-engine training in the AT-10. He was promoted to Flight Officer and assigned to Air Transport Command.

Romie was then sent to Love Field in Dallas to get his shots for overseas assignment. Instead, he was sent to Kansas City to an aircraft factory and assigned to ferry B-25's to Romulus, Mich. These twin engine bombers were delivered to the Russians at Romulus already painted with the red star of Russia.

Romie then made his first trip overseas when he was assigned to deliver a C-46 to Biak, off the coast of New Guinea in the South Pacific. This was late 1944. He then returned to Nashville, Tenn. to prepare for assignment to the European war zone. Instead, he was sent to Hollandia, New Guinea for transport service. There he flew C-47's to transport whatever needed to be moved - Red Cross personnel, POW's, lumber, etc. When Leyte was secured in the Philippines, he was sent there and remained until the war ended.

Romie received his discharge at Ft. Sam Houston in Texas shortly after the war ended. He had about 4000 flight hours, never had a crash, and never had to bail out of a plane. He never shot at the enemy and was never shot at by the enemy.

Romie was in the service over three years, passed his flying skills on to other youngsters to become instructors and combat pilots. He did everything he was called on to do and served his country well in time of need.

PT-17 trainer.

THE GOLFER

When I moved to Atlanta, Ga. in 1958, I was told by a friend to look up a fellow by the name of Earl Fleenor if I wanted a golfing companion. I had played a few games of golf and I was getting too old to continue playing amateur baseball, so I contacted Earl. At that time I was working 5-1/2 days a week on the railroad. My half day to work was on Sunday so Earl and I played golf every Saturday. I found out that Earl loved his golf about as well as anyone could love a sport, and he taught me to also love the game. We had many good matches together but Earl nearly always won.

Like almost everyone else from my generation, Earl served his country during World War II. He was from Bristol, Tenn. and was drafted on November 16, 1942. He was inducted at Ft. Oglethorpe, Ga., just outside Chattanooga, Tenn. Ft. Oglethorpe had been a Calvary post during World War I. That old military base is now gone.

Earl was shipped out to Miami Beach, Fla. for basic training. Earl remembers that he had two Thanksgiving dinners that year - one on the train and the other after he arrived at Miami Beach. He said there were 90,000 Air Force personnel at Miami Beach at that time. They were put up in one of those fancy hotels with six to a room and no hot water. He was there about 3 months.

Earl was then shipped to Louisiana State University in Baton Rouge, La. where he was assigned to an Army Administration School. This was a school for learning how to prepare military forms and handle military correspondence. The men were quartered in rooms built into the football stadium with four to a room.

After the schooling at LSU, Earl was shipped to DeRidder, La. where they were just completing a new air base. Earl was assigned to the 350th Army Air Force Medical Corps and the hospital was not quite completed.

The hospital was finished in a short time and the group moved in, where Earl remained for almost two years. The Base Surgeon took a liking to Earl and his work, and being one of the lucky ones - he was never shipped out. Earl got married in December 1944 and he and his wife had a small apartment in town. Earl's group helped shut the base down before he was moved to Stuttgart, Ark.

Since Earl was married, he was assigned a small apartment on the base. The couple enjoyed their stay in Stuttgart. Earl on occasions was able to play golf at the Colonial Country Club in Memphis and the Little Rock Country Club. Earl said those two clubs were nice to servicemen and they were able to play free. In

Earl Fleenor and Sam.

December 1945, it was decided to close the base down in Stuttgart. Earl learned that he would be released from the service in a couple of months, so he went on furlough and took his wife back to Bristol, Tenn.

He then reported to Barksdale Field in Shreveport, La. where he was discharged on Feb. 18, 1946. Earl's discharge papers showed he hid served 3 years, 3 months, and 3 days. Earl was a Staff Sergeant. During his service Earl saw parts of the country he had not seen before, became a married man, and became a veteran who had served his country as he was called on to do.

Earl Fleenor celebrated his 80th birthday in December of 1996.

THE ISLAND HOPPER

I have played many rounds of golf with Bill Owens and, when I asked him about his World War II experience, he quickly told me that he was an island hopper.

Bill was raised in Norfolk, Va. and he was drafted in December of 1942. He was assigned to the Air Corps and sent to Atlantic City, N. J. for basic training. At that time, Atlantic City was not the gambling mecca that it is today.

After basic training Bill was sent to Omaha, Neb. where he received radio signal training for aviation. From there he was sent to Hammer Field in California for advanced communications training. Then he was ready for overseas duty with the B-24 bomber command of the 13th Army Air Corps.

Bill was first sent to Kola Field on Guadalcanal which had just been taken from the Japanese in Feb. of 1943. Bill said there were still a few Japanese hid out in some of the caves when they arrived. From Guadalcanal the B-24's were able to strike targets in many areas of the South Pacific. Bill handled coded messages and strike data for both the army and the navy.

By June of 1943 the U.S. forces had moved 170 miles northwest of Guadalcanal into the New Georgia Islands and flight operations were moved to Mundi. They moved to Bougainville by November of 1943. From there they bombed Rabaul in the New Britain Islands, always moving northwest toward Japan.

The airfield at Hollandia in New Guinea was captured in April of 1944 and the bomber group moved there. The airfield in the Admiralty Islands was also secured in April and the bomber group moved again. At this location the Japanese were only two miles away and our forces were frequently

Consolidated B-24 Liberators.

Bill says that the communication crews usually were moved in the C-47 transport planes but now and then they would get to ride on the B-24. On such trips they would usually drop their bombs on some target enroute. They would often move to a new island location and set up communications on the air strip even before the island was completely taken.

By November of 1944 the bomber group had moved to the Marianas. From this location the big B-29's were able to raid Japan with deadly force.

The Philippines were retaken from the Japanese and Manila was liberated in Feb. of 1945. As the war drew to a close in the Pacific, Bill was sent to Clark Field at Manila. He was later sent back to the states with sufficient points to get out of service. He was discharged at Ft. Brag, N. C.

Bill was right...he was an island hopper.

THE FRENCH HORN

I first met Earle Luck (by letter) while doing a study of family history. Earle and I were both on a mailing list to receive the Dabbs Newsletter, which I later inherited.

Earle graduated from high school in 1944 and immediately tried to volunteer for military service. Because of poor eyesight he was told that he could not volunteer but he would probably be drafted when he reached age. That summer, when he reached 18, he registered for the draft and volunteered for immediate induction. While waiting to be called, he took a post graduate course, mostly to play in the band. He soon tired of that and took a job in a defense plant making electrical resistance thermometer bulbs for airplanes. In the meantime, Earle had been receiving draft card classifications, a new one almost every month, ranging from 4F to 1A, and numerous in-betweens.

Earle then went to the draft board and asked what he had to do to get in. They suggested volunteering for immediate induction. When they learned that he had already done that, they suggested he try again. This time he was accepted on what he later learned was the last draft from that board.

Earle went to Fort Dix, N. J. and, after a series of tests, he was told that he would be in the Army band, and would go to Langley Field, Va. for basic training. Instead, he was sent to San Antonio, Tex. (IDACC), which had to do with indoctrination at the air training center for Air Force basic training, near Kelly Field.

From there Earle was sent to band school in Washington, D. C. which Earle states was so overcrowded that they hoped no one would turn up for rehearsals. After a visit home for Christmas, Earle was sent to the 745th Army Air Force Band, at 15th Air Force Headquarters in Colorado Springs, Colorado. The main job there was to go to nearby Peterson Field whenever a general came in, only to learn the general had flown in during the night.

The band also rehearsed and played on Sundays when the camp was quarantined due to a flu epidemic. By that time, they were able to wear civilian clothes when off duty and, there being no fence around the camp, the camp was deserted despite the quarantine. The band had rehearsals every morning and went into town at night. Earle not only played French Horn (hard to find) but also played guitar in the dance orchestra. He was promised sergeant stripes if he would re-enlist.

There were all kinds of rumors that Earle's unit was going to be moved, and some rumors were to less desirable spots. Earle decided that living in doubt as to where he might go, and when, wasn't for him, and he was the last draftee to be released from that camp.

Earle Luck.

While there, as bandsmen subject to calls at any time to meet incoming generals at the airfield, the band did not have to serve on KP duty (kitchen police). They made up for this by playing at the men's mess hall one day each week, one day at the women's mess hall, and one day at the mess hall at Peterson Field.

At the end of seven months and 25 days, Earle was discharged in Denver and flew home, the first flight of his life, even though he had served in the Air Force. Back in civilian life, Earle found he was eligible for the American Legion, but not the VFW. He got some benefits from the GI Bill, and a VA loan later helped buy his first home.

THE HOSPITAL CORPSMAN

Phil Mobbs is one of the better players in our seniors golf group, and a veteran of World War II.

He was born in Massachusetts and was drafted in June of 1943, but elected to go in the Navy. After completion of boot camp at Newport, RI he was sent to Portsmouth, Va. to a hospital corps school.

After Phil finished his schooling in Portsmouth, he was classified as a Hospital Corpsman and sent to Philadelphia, Pa. where he worked in the hospital. From there he went to Atlantic City, N. J. to the air station dispensary. Once again he returned to the Naval Hospital in Philadelphia. From there he was sent to Camp Allen in Norfolk, Va., which at that time was an amphibious training base. Phil was then sent to Lido Beach in Long Island, N.Y and was later sent to Shoemaker, Calif. where a receiving station was located. From there he was moved to Oceanside, Calif. for special training in what was called a "Beach Party". This phase of training was a program to learn all of the things that go along with an assault landing, such as moving in supplies, putting up medical flags on the beach, treating and evacuating the wounded, moving the casualties, etc. Phil was now ready for the real task that lay ahead.

Phil was sent to Astoria, Oregon where he was assigned to the *USS Logan*, APA-196. It was now October 1944. They sailed to Pearl Harbor and from there to Saipan which was a staging area for the assault on Iwo Jima. Saipan had been taken from the Japanese only a few months earlier in a battle that lasted from June 16th until July 9, 1944, and which cost the United States 10,000 casualties. Saipan was one of the more important islands in the Marianas group.

The *USS Logan* went with the assault force that landed on Iwo on February 19, 1945. Between 30,000 and 40,000 combat troops went to Iwo in an armada of 300 ships. Phil went on shore about 5AM the morning after initial landings were made. In the first 58 hours there were 643 Americans killed, 550 missing, and 4,168 were wounded. Phil, and the members of his party, really had their hands full to perform the tasks they had been trained to do. There were piles of dead Marines and wounded everywhere. The wounded were evacuated at night and many dead were buried at sea. The *USS Logan* rammed another vessel while operating at night and severely damaged the bow of the ship. They were able to seal off the damaged area and continued with their work. The ships medical compliment had been greatly increased in anticipation of large numbers of casualties. The troop compartments recently occupied by fresh invasion troops, were now occupied by the casualties of war - hundreds of them. The medical personnel -.were overwhelmed. Even with surgeons operating around the clock, the injuries of many were so severe they did not survive. Probably as many as 4,000 Americans died in the battle for Iwo Jima.

Phil was witness to the flag being raised over Mt. Suribachi, which was a memorable incident that led to a monument being constructed in the Washington, D. C. area later on.

The *USS Logan* then went back to Guam where the wounded were offloaded to a hospital. Guam was an island that had been taken by the Japanese only three days after they bombed Pearl Harbor. The battle to recapture the island by the U. S. had lasted from July 20, 1944 until August 8, 1944. It had been a major task but casualties were not as great as on Saipan which had fallen to the U. S. a few days earlier.

The *USS Logan*, although damaged, then returned to Saipan for additional training exercises in preparation for the invasion of Okinawa. The time came for their departure and they participated in the 1400 ship armada that bore down on Okinawa. With heavy shelling from the fleet, the Japanese abandoned their strong coastal positions and moved inland. The initial landings on April 1, 1945 met with little resistance but would later meet strong resistance as they moved onland. The small boats from the *USS Logan* made several dummy runs toward the coast before moving away. This was done to help confuse the enemy as to where the landings would actually occur. Phil was riding in one of these small boats which were bombarded continuously by the Japanese shore batteries throughout the false landing runs.

During the operation against Okinawa, the small islands in the Ryukyus chain just west of Okinawa were also invaded by American troops. The conquest of this group of small islands resulted in the capture of more than 300 "suicide" boats, which were small boats designed by the Japanese to ram American ships.

The *USS Logan* stayed at Okinawa for several days but, due to the small number of casualties initially, and the fact that their ship needed repairs, they returned to Saipan. They were then ordered to New Caledonia for repairs to the bow of the ship. Repairs were completed in about six weeks.

Atomic bombs were dropped on Japan in August of 1945 to end the war. The *USS Logan* was ordered to Wakayama, Japan as part of the occupation force. They remained on the beach there for about a week. Phil said the Japanese people were scared to death of the Americans and probably thought they were monsters. Phil said it was the children who first came out and made friends with the sailors and later on the older people abandoned their fears. The innocence and the smiles of the very young once again showed what life on this planet should be like for all mankind.

The *USS Logan* was then ordered back to the United States with a stop in the Philippines to pick up returning troops. They landed in Seattle, Washington, and were back home again with the completion of a war that truly showed the inhumanity of man, but had to be done by the United States.

Phil remained in the U.S. Navy for 30 years and retired in 1973. He rose through the ranks to become a Lt. Commander, quite an accomplishment for an enlisted man.

THE MEDAL OF HONOR

Several months after the Japanese bombed Pearl Harbor in December of 1941, 1 joined the Naval Air Corps. I was sent to the University of Cincinnati for a Navy program called V-5. The program included classes at the university and flight training at a private airport on the outskirts of town. Bud Norton, at 18, was the youngest member of our group. Bud and I were together in Cincinnati and at the University of Iowa for pre-flight training, and later for flight training in Minneapolis, Minn. That was the last time I saw Bud until after the war in 1947.

A few years ago I contacted Bud at his home in Michigan and we exchanged phone calls a few times. Bud recently called and wanted to know if he could stop in for a short visit and I was delighted to see him again for the first time in fifty years. During his short visit he shared with me a little known story that was very interesting.

Bud Norton had a distinguished career as a pilot during World War II and remained in the Naval Reserve after the war. He was called back to active duty during the Korean War and was stationed at Norfolk, Va. for a short time. One day he was sent out in his plane to observe and make contact with a submarine performing some test exercises. On his flight back to Norfolk Bud observed a destroyer and a tanker down below. The destroyer made a sharp turn in front of the tanker and the tanker rammed the destroyer. The destroyer caught on fire and Bud could see men jumping into the sea and swimming around in the water. He got in touch with the base and reported the accident, then flew around over the scene until his gas supply dictated that he return to base. He had done all he could do. Bud was later transferred to an aircraft carrier for duty in the Mediterranean. Many months later a Lt. Commander was assigned to the carrier squadron and Bud observed that the new officer had very few flight hours for an officer of that grade. He asked the Lt. Commander why he had such few hours and the young officer told how it came about.

He said he had been on a destroyer off the coast of Virginia when they were rammed by a tanker and the destroyer caught on fire. When the tanker backed away from the destroyer, a number of men were sucked into the ocean. He was a Chief Petty Officer at that time and he was one of those men. He told Bud that there were a large number of men in the water and he got them together and they swim to the far side of the destroyer, away from the fire, boarded the ship and put out the fire. For this action he received the Medal of Honor and was promoted to the rank of Lt. Commander. Then the Navy asked what he would like to do next and he told them he had always wanted to fly. The Navy sent him to flight school and from there to the aircraft carrier. That was why he, as a Lt. Commander, had very few flight hours.

Bud then told him that he was the pilot who circled overhead after the accident occurred, and he was glad the men and the destroyer had been saved.

THE SKIPPER

Harry Cummings was raised in the Ocean View section of Norfolk, Va.
He was the son of a Navy officer who had worked his way up through the
ranks. After high school Harry spent one year in the Navy Reserve and then
took the exam for entrance to the U.S. Naval Academy in Annapolis, Md. At
that time the Academy would accept 15 sons of armed forces personnel into
the Academy based on competitive scores from the applicants. Harry was
one of the fortunate fifteen to be accepted. He was in school at the Naval
Academy when the Japanese struck Pearl Harbor in December of 1941.
Harry graduated in 1943 and received his commission as an Ensign in the
United States Navy.

As a young Ensign, Harry Cummings spent a few weeks at torpedo school
in Casco Bay, Maine before being assigned to the *USS Ericsson*, a destroyer
assigned to escort convoys across the Atlantic. The convoys were turned
over to the British upon arrival at Gibraltar. The *Ericsson* had numerous
encounters with German submarines but had no confirmed kills. Harry was
assigned as Assistant Gunnery Officer.

One night, while on convoy duty in the Atlantic, the *Ericsson* was struck
by a tremendous wave that tilted the ship 45 degrees. It was not known
immediately as to what had happened. General quarters was sounded and a
muster taken. It was found that the sailor on security watch was missing.
The following morning the sailor was picked up by another ship. It was then
learned that the young sailor had been washed overboard when the big wave
struck the ship. He had survived several hours in the water by holding on to
a piece of wood and later found a floater net, which he was able to climb on.
The sailor could not swim, but he had survived.

In early 1944 the *Ericsson*, together with the *USS Kearny*, were assigned
to escort the Heavy Cruiser Brooklyn on duty in the Mediterranean. There

In early 1944 the *Ericsson*, together with the *USS Kearny*, were assigned to escort the Heavy Cruiser Brooklyn on duty in the Mediterranean. There they performed anti-submarine work and participated in shore bombardments, In an attempt to outflank the German defenses in southern Italy, U.S. forces landed at Anzio on January 22, 1944. The Germans surrounded the 50,000 U. S. troops, who withstood a four-month siege of their beachhead. The *Brooklyn*, the *Kearny*, and the *Ericsson* made numerous bombardments of the German positions but would have to pull back when the Germans turned their heavy guns in their direction.

The Allies invaded France in June of 1944 and also advanced into Rome, Italy about the same time. On August 15th a huge Allied force landed in southern France between Toulon and Cannes. The *USS Ericsson* served as an escort ship for the troops who made this landing. The *Ericsson* continued to patrol the coast after the landings were made. A few nights later, south of Toulon, the *Ericsson* picked something up on radar. Investigation discovered the object was an open boat filled with German sailors. There were about 20 men crowded in the boat and they were the crew of a German submarine that had been abandoned in the harbor at Toulon. They were trying to escape the invading forces.

The *Ericsson* was then ordered back to the states and Harry spent a few weeks at a gunnery school in Washington, D. C. The *Ericsson* was then sent to Pearl Harbor and later assigned to carry occupation forces to Japan when peace was declared in the Pacific. By that time Harry had reached the rank of Lieutenant.

With the war at an end, Harry Cummings decided to remain in the Navy and later rose to the rank of Captain. His first assignment as Commanding Officer was on the *LSMR 517* (a rocket launcher landing ship). He was then assigned as Captain of the destroyer *USS Waldron*. And, finally, he was Captain of the missile cruiser *USS Josephus Daniels*. Harry retired in 1972 after 30 years in the service of his country.

THE DUKE

Doran Ford, a golfing friend, was born in West Virginia. Like other high school youngsters during World War 11, he was anxious to enlist in the service. He tried to get his father to sign for him when he reached age 17 but his father wanted him to stay in school. Doran stayed in school another year and by that time the war was winding down in the Pacific. Doran's older brother had been in the U.S. Navy since 1932 and was at Pearl Harbor when bombed by the Japanese.

Doran said everyone in his county had a nickname and his was 'Duke', a name he still carries. His best friend was called 'Pickle'. Pickle wanted to enlist in the navy in 1945 but the nearest recruiting station was in Clarksburg, W. Va. Pickle told Duke he didn't know where the recruiting station was located in Clarksburg and Duke volunteered to go with Pickle and help him find the place.

Duke and Pickle went to Clarksburg, found the recruiting station, and Pickle took the eye examination. He was turned down immediately and was told that he was "blind as a bat". Duke said he would never forget the recruiting officer in Clarksburg as "he was really a slick talker". He asked Duke why he didn't take the eye test since he was there, so he did. This led from one thing to another and before Duke knew it, he was in the U.S. Navy at age 18.

Duke was sent to Great Lakes for basic training and from there to San Diego for Yeoman's School. By then the war with Japan had ended and Duke was sent to Washington, D. C. for a time.

After the war ended, Duke signed up for submarine school, hoping to be assigned to the same submarine with his brother who had gone through the war safely and had no real complaints except for the poor quality of the torpedoes they were using.

THE ATHLETE

Bill Roughton was born in Norfolk, Va. and was in high school when the war started in 1941. Like so many other youngsters at that time, becoming a pilot in the Air Corps was very appealing. Bill was very active in high school sports. He was voted All State in basketball as well as baseball, and was first string end for two years on the football team.

When Bill reached age 17, he enlisted in the Air Corps cadet program. At that time young cadets were not being called to active duty until age 18, so Bill was able to finish high school. He graduated in January of 1945. Bill was called to

Bill Roughton. Salt Lake City, 1945.

duty in Feb. 1945 and sent to Keesler Field in Biloxi, Miss. for basic training. By that time the cadet program was overflowing and most hopeful cadets ended up on other assignments.

During the war many of the military schools and bases had baseball and football teams... some even had basketball teams. These teams often played the Naval Academy and West Point. Some of these teams were good enough to play against professional teams. Many of these military teams had players who had entered service from professional baseball teams and from other sports. Because Bill was good in sports, he played on the basketball team at

Keesler Field. Later on, these youngsters who were unable to go on to pilot training were given some choices as to where they might like to go. Bill selected Salt Lake City, Utah.

There were two air bases in Salt Lake City and Bill arrived at Salt Lake City Air Base in October 1945. He was there only a short time when the base was closed and Bill moved over to Kerns Field, still in Salt Lake City. Bill was assigned to Special Services where he mostly processed personnel for transfer to the West Coast in preparation for going to the South Pacific. While there Bill played on their baseball team and they participated in a semi-pro league. Bill had good duty in Salt Lake City for about a year.

He learned that he was to be discharged so he came home on furlough in September 1946 and registered for college. He then reported to Ft. Meade, Md. and received his discharge in October 1946.

Bill and I are in the same golf group at Virginia Beach. He told me he enjoyed his time in the service, learned a lot, and it meant a lot in his growing up process.

THE SHIP BUILDER

Leo Midgett is a member of our senior golf group and we have often played golf together. He was born in South Norfolk, Va.

When World War 11 started, Leo was working in the ship yard, He was deferred until August of 1944 because he was working in a defense related industry. When he learned that he was to be drafted, he enlisted in the Navy and was sent to Bainbridge, Md. for boot camp.

Leo was then sent to Mare Island, Calif. where he was assigned to the ship yard doing practically the same thing he had been doing before he entered the service only for much less pay.

Leo worked his way up to Fireman 2nd Class. At the ship yard, he helped build the *USS Neurus*, a Submarine Tender. The war had just about ended when the ship was finished and went to sea. Leo not only helped build the *USS Neurus* but also went with the ship on its first voyage. The *Neurus* went to Japan as part of the occupation force and was stationed at Sasebo, Japan.

Leo Midgett.

Servicemen were not allowed to drink Japanese water and when they went on shore, they always carried their canteen of water with them. Canteens are fitted into a canvas pouch which make it easy to carry. Men often cut the sides out of the canteen in order to fill them with cigarettes. The cigarettes were then used to trade for Japanese goods and services. He said the sailors could get almost anything they wanted with their cigarettes, but most of the time they were traded for souvenirs to take home.

The Japanese were said to have never showed any outward animosity toward the Americans. One could be in a bar and leave his money on the table while he went to the dance floor

Japanese Pile Driver, Sasebo Japan. January 1946.

or the bathroom... it was never bothered.

Leo had a Japanese girlfriend and he took her to the Petty Officer's club one night for dinner. A 16 ounce steak with baked potato cost about $1.70, but his girl friend only ordered a bowl of rice.

Japanese men would often get in their boat and come out to the ship. They would clean and scrub the entire ship for a few bowls of rice as their pay. A pot of rice was always on the stove to pay the Japanese for their work.

Sasebo was a major port for the Japanese but the machine shops and other shops for ship repair were located in caves back in the side of the mountain.

The men were on duty three days and were off every third day, but they were only allowed on shore every six days. This meant that every other off day they could not go on shore. If they stayed on board the ship, they had to work. On the other hand, they could go to a place in the bay called "The Pimple", a rock location. There, they were permitted to drink their allotted two cans of beer and they wouldn't have to stay on board the ship and work. Leo said he never cared much for beer until it was the key to being off ship and not having to work.

Leo got out of the Navy in April of 1946 but stayed in the Reserve. He was called back to active duty during the Korean War and remained in the Navy until 1965, and the completion of 16 years in the service of his country.

He is the only person I ever knew to have two holes-in-one in the game of golf on the same day.

DESTINATION EGYPT

Bill Marsh was my childhood friend and school buddy. When we graduated in 1937, Bill followed in the footsteps of his father and became a foundry patternmaker. When the war started in Dec. of 1941 Bill was working in Hamilton, Ohio and could have stayed out of military service as his job was essential to the war effort. None the less, he immediately left his job and returned home in Chattanooga, Tenn. to volunteer for service.

Bill Marsh really wanted in the Navy but was turned down on his physical, because of an imperfection in his teeth that would not permit him to wear a gas mask. He tried to get in the Marines, the Air Force, and the Amy, but was turned down each time.

Over looking Jerusalem. June 25, 1943. Bill Marsh is third from right, front row.

He refused to give up and finally, after several months had gone by, he was accepted by the Amy and sent to Aberdeen, Md. where he was assigned to the 303rd Medium Artillery Group. After a few months in training he was sent to Newport News, Va. where he and 7500 other troops boarded a ship, destination unknown. This was Oct. 7, 1942.

After a stop in Rio de Janeiro to pick up supplies, they sailed to South Africa where they were allowed off ship for one day in Durban. They then sailed through the channel at Madagascar, up the east coast of Africa, into the Red Sea and arrived at the entrance to the Suez Canal. They disembarked there on Dec. 12, 1942. There, they

Bill Marsh.

boarded a train for Cairo, Egypt where they set up camp 20 miles from the city. Tents stretched as far as one could see and there were four men in each tent.

Bill and his companions had no way of knowing but they were probably part of a plan called Operation Torch, planned in July, and implemented as a combined British and U.S. Army of 400,000 men which landed in French North Africa on Nov. 8th. The plan called for these troops to advance eastward, while General Montgomery kept pressing the German forces westward from Egypt. By the time Bill arrived in Egypt, Montgomery had unleashed a great drive against the Germans that resulted in a break-through on Nov. 3rd. By Nov. 7th Rommel was in full retreat 240 miles west of El Alamein. That ended his planned conquest of Egypt.

During his many months in the Cairo area, Bill and his comrades picked up many damaged tanks in the desert and brought them in for repairs. One of his most memorable experiences of Egypt was to see the pyramids and the other wonders of Egypt. He also well remembers participating in a truck convoy of 150 trucks from Cairo to Hamadan, Persia (now Iran). Their route took them through Syria and Iraq (formerly Mesopotamia). Bill was a non smoker, but he remembers selling his own cigarettes at considerable profit in Baghdad.

Bill, a Sergeant, was later transferred back to the states and assigned to a military police outfit in Memphis, Tenn. From there he was sent to Rupert, Idaho where German prisoners were being held. He was only there for about two weeks before being moved to Salt Lake City and receiving his discharge in June of 1945.

THE USS ALHENA

My good friend Fred Hockert was born in Minnesota. He enlisted in the U.S. Navy in 1938 at age 17. He served for a short time on the Heavy Cruiser USS Salt Lake City, and then spent about two years at the Naval Air Station in San Diego. He was later assigned to the USS Alhena. AK-26, a cargo ship put in service in 1941 prior to the Japanese attack at Pearl Harbor. They made several trips to Newfoundland, Iceland and the British Isles and were back in Norfolk, Va. when the war started in December. They made one more trip to Argentia, Newfoundland before getting orders for the South Pacific. Enroute to the Pacific, they stopped at the Tonga Islands and participated in the initial operations against Guadalcanal which started on August 7, 1942.

During later stages of the Solomons campaign, the *USS Alhena* delivered cargo to Tulagi- across the bay from Guadalcanal. That same evening the destroyer *USS Blue* was sunk on the way in to Tulagi. *USS Alhena* left Tulagi about midnight and a short time later was struck by a Japanese torpedo. The destroyer *USS Monson* was sunk about the same time. This was in September of 1942. There were 33 people on the *Alhena* who were killed by the explosion. Many of those killed were mentally sick Marines that had been taken an board. There were several Japanese prisoners also on board. One young sailor lost a leg in the explosion and he was so angry and in such pain, he yelled and screamed at the Skipper to give him a gun so he could kill the Japanese prisoners. He survived only a few hours.

Thinking that the ship was going down, the crew abandoned ship. The stern of the ship went under water but the ship did not go down. With its water-tight bulkheads closed, the ship was able to stay afloat. The crew got back on the ship the following morning and buried the dead.

The tug *Navajo* took over and towed the *Alhena* to New Hebrides. When

Fred and Vera Hockert. Vera is an Australian girl and they were married during World War II.

they arrived there, they found that the Japanese had just bombed several ships in the harbor with considerable damage. They remained in New Hebrides for three days before being towed on to Australia. Upon arrival in Sydney they were just in time to see a Japanese submarine sink a ferry boat in the harbor.

The *Alhena* remained in Australia for seven months being repaired and work was finally completed in June 1943. During the seven months in Australia, Fred and other shipmates found girl friends who would later become their wives.

After repairs were completed, the *Alhena* went to New Zealand, picked up Marines and took them to Bougainville where they participated in initial landings there. The *Alhena* was under attack several times but received no damage.

The *USS Alhena* later returned to Guadalcanal and while there word came down that permission had been received from the Fleet Admiral for some of the men to return to Australia to be married. Thirty eight members of the crew flew from Guadalcanal on a B-17 bomber to Brisbane, Australia where Fred rode the train to Sydney and was married in April of 1944. Fred remained in Australia for 73 days before shipping out to Pearl Harbor on the troop ship *USS President Johnson*. There he served in the Headquarters of the Amphibious Fleet for about one year. He was then transferred to Washington, D. C. and was stationed at the Naval Research Lab until the war ended.

In the mean time, the *USS Alhena* participated in the operation against Saipan without crew member Fred Heckert. She then returned to the United States for overhaul. Returning to the South Pacific in early November, the *Alhena* was at Manus Inland where she was damaged in the explosion of the ammunition ship *USS Mount Hood*. The *Alhena* was close by when the explosion occurred and several of Fred's former officers and shipmates were killed. The *Alhena* was out of service for about six nooks for repairs and then participated in the liberation of the Philippines in early 1945. She proceeded to Guam where she loaded for the impending operations against Iwo Jima. Following the Iwo operation, the *Alhena* made numerous trips between various islands before the war ended and she was employed in the initial occupation of Japan. Fred was in charge of administration while on the *Alhena*. He stayed in the Navy for 23 years and retired in 1961 as Chief Yeoman.

A PLACE THAT TESTED MEN'S SOULS

Over fifty years ago on August 7, 1942 the great battle for Guadalcanal took place in the Solomon Islands. This was the first U. S. offensive in the Pacific Theater following the Japanese attack on Pearl Harbor. The battle for the island lasted six months before it was finally taken from the Japanese in February, 1943. For those of us old enough to remember, those were trying times as it appeared that the next step for the Japanese was to launch an attack on Australia from an airfield being built on Guadalcanal. Guadalcanal was said to be "A place that tested men's souls", It was not just a place where men on the land battled for possession of the island, it was also a place where the seas in the area were filled with ships as each side tried to supply and reinforce their soldiers fighting for the island. More than 40 ships lie on the ocean floor in the waters around Guadalcanal. Fifty years ago, 82 ships and 18,000 Marines started the battle for Guadalcanal. The United States lost 1,769 ground troops, 4,911 men at sea and 420 in the air. The Japanese lost over 30,000 men. The Marines learned difficult lessons in jungle fighting and it was here that boys became men. It was here that many brave young men gave their lives for the freedom that we enjoy today. Some of my friends were involved in the fighting for Guadalcanal. On anniversary dates of that great battle, they relive memories of those trying times and often shed a tear for young friends that were left behind.

THE CRASH LANDING

Hal Lamb was my high school classmate and a star on the football team. In January of 1942, after war was declared, he enlisted in the Amy Air Corps.

Like other cadets in pilot training, Hal was moved around quite a bit. He had primary flight training at Camden, S. C., basic pilot training at Sumter, S. C., and advanced training at Moody Field in Valdosta, Ga. He was later sent to Sebring, Fla. for training in the B-17, four engine bomber. Later on he was sent to Ephrata, Wash. and became part of the 398th Bomb Group. In mid 1943, Hal moved to Rapid City, S. D. and trained B-17 crews.

The 398th Bomb Group of 72 B-17's flew to England in early 1944 and became the last group to join the 8th Air Force. Hal was credited with 39 missions over enemy territory. He commented, "Our record was commendable but no more so than other like units." This was typical of Hal and a very modest assessment by a man who flew in harm's way day after day in raids over France and Germany. Their missions included raids to such places as Berlin, Leipzig, Ludwigshaven, Wiesbaden, multiple missile launch sites and many very busy missions during the invasion in June of 1944.

Hal described his activities as follows: "My war experiences were not of particular note; consisting primarily of ongoing suspense interrupted by occasional periods of sheer terror." Such was the life of a bomber pilot in the skies over Germany, who had to face flak from the ground and German fighter planes in the skies.

The most tiresome mission he flew was when he participated in a thousand plane raid over the eastern most missile research center in Germany. It was a mission that lasted over 13 hours but hopefully delayed their research.

Hal was grateful they arrived in England after the P-51 fighter plane was well established. The P-51 was capable of long range escort service and able to protect the big bombers on their missions into the heart of Germany. He once saw three P-51's take on what seemed a sky full of German fighters. He said the P-51's came across his nose, dropping their extra fuel tanks, and made the Germans scuttle for home. Hal said he would always happily treat drinks for the "Fighter Jocks". A few months before the 398th Bomb Group arrived in England, and the development of the P-31 fighter, the 8th Air Force would often lose 30 or more bombers in a single day.

Hal flew a lot of missions during the invasion of Normandy in June of 1944. At that time their targets were along the coast and not more than 50 miles inland.

On one mission against a missile site in France, three of their 12 planes were shot down by flak and Hal's plane lost three engines. After throwing every loose item overboard and dismantling the ball turret, they

Capt. Hal Lamb.

were able to nurse the one remaining engine into providing enough power to enable a glide across the channel. They landed on the beach without mishap, skidded to a stop and evacuated posthaste. A gent atop the bluff shouted that they were in a mine field. Hal and the crew froze and remained in suspense until they were escorted from danger. This was written up in local newspapers at that time, with the headline reading: "CAPT. HAL LAMB LANDS CRIPPLED FORTRESS IN MINEFIELD - BARELY!!"

Hal remained in the service after the war and retired in 1971 with 30 years service. He now lives in Texas. Hal attained the rank of Colonel.

THE CONDUCTOR

Back during World War II, I spent a few months at a small town in Alabama called Courtland. Courtland is so small that even today it is not shown on most road maps. During the war , a large bomber base was located there. I had completed basic training in the Army Air Corps and had been sent to Courtland to await entry into Pre-Flight training at Maxwell Field in Montgomery, Ala.

Courtland was located on Southern Railway's main line that ran from Chattanooga, Tenn. to Memphis, Tenn. Since I was on leave from the railroad, I was able to get free transportation on the railroad, but each time I wanted to travel I had to order a pass from the office in Cincinnati, Ohio. This was a bit inconvenient since I never knew how long I would stay at one of these military installations.

Occasionally I would get a week-end pass from the military and ride the local train to Chattanooga to visit mom and dad. On my first trip home I found out that the question of transportation was not going to be a problem.

On my first trip from Courtland to Chattanooga and return, the conductor asked me if I was going home and I told him I was. He told me to keep my pass as I might want to use it again.

I was only in Courtland a short time before being sent to Montgomery, Ala. for three months. From Montgomery, I was sent to Decatur, Ala. for flight training. Decatur was also located on Southern Railway's main line, and just a few miles east of Courtland.

When I arrived in Decatur, I still had my railroad pass I had used when I was in Courtland. Once again I was able to ride the local train to Chattanooga, with the same conductor, and using the same pass I had used when I had been in Courtland.

I still remember the old gentleman who was the conductor on that train and how nice he was to me. He made his job pleasant by being friendly with all of the passengers. I can still picture his face and his conductor's uniform with shiny brass buttons and the little bill-cap he wore on his head.

Somehow he knew I was just a kid in a topsy-turvy world torn apart by the war, going home to see someone I loved. He might have had kids of his own out there somewhere, but somehow he knew that little piece of paper I held in my hand was important to me and maybe I would get another chance to visit home. He was a kind old gentleman and I shall always remember him.

NAVAL ACADEMY GRADUATE

Ted Roderick is a member of our senior golf group at Virginia Beach, Va. When he graduated from high school in Ohio, Ted thought he had an opportunity to get in the United States Naval Academy at Annapolis. He was later told that it would cost $500 to be appointed by a Congressman in another state who had an appointment available. Since this was illegal, Ted decided he would take a competitive exam, which he won and was accepted by the Naval Academy in 1937. He picked up the story as follows:

" The first intimation of trouble occurred when I was a midshipman at Annapolis and had just completed two years of service. My classmates and I (class of '41) were assembled in Memorial Hall and told by the Commandant that the world was heading for increasingly uncertain times and that we could resign now if we so desired, but if we started our third year, we would be in for the duration. (None of us resigned.) The second occurred when our summer cruise that was scheduled to go to Europe was changed to a South American

U. S. S. DUPONT

cruise including Rio was further changed to going only as far south as Caracas, Venezuela because of German ships operating in the South Atlantic. The third occurred when graduation date was accelerated from June of 1941 to February of 1941 to get us into the fleet quicker.

I reported aboard the destroyer *DuPont* (DD 152) based in Norfolk, Va. about March 1st. After a month or two of customary naval exercises, the *DuPont* and other destroyers in her division started northward under orders - first to Philadelphia, then New York and finally Boston. About this time, the destroyer tender, *Prairie*, moved to Argentia Bay, Newfoundland, anchored there and established a destroyer base. We proceeded from Boston to Argentia and nested alongside the *Prairie* where we remained for a week or so. Shortly after this, another base was established in one of the fjords of Iceland, ten or fifteen miles north of Reykjavik.

With two destroyer bases now established in the North Atlantic, a certain routine began, to escort convoys from Canada to England. A convoy of fully loaded merchant ships would a assemble on the East Coast (Halifax perhaps). The convoy would form into eight to ten columns of eight to ten ships in each column and all headed eastward towards England. Thus, there were about sixty to a hundred ships in each convoy; and if I had to guess, I would guess that there were weekly convoy sailings. Canadian destroyers or 'corvettes' would escort the convoy to a few hundred miles south of Argentia, Newfoundland and at a prescribed meeting place would turn over escort duties to the Americans. President Roosevelt had declared that we (the United States) would be escorting American naval ships between Newfoundland and Iceland and that any other ships were eligible for our protection while we were doing so. So four or five American destroyers would escort an American oilier or cargo ship to the rendezvous where we would meet sixty to a hundred British merchant ships. We would then proceed to another point about four hundred miles south of Iceland where we would rendezvous with four or five English destroyers. We would turn over escort duties to the English and we would escort our one or two American naval vessels up to Iceland. I believe it was about August or September that we established these bases at Argentia and Hvalfjordur and at first they were just two destroyer tenders, one at each location -but these soon expanded into good sized facilities on land to take care of the fighting ships.

It seems to me that we started escorting convoys about August or September. I imagine the mix of escorting vessels was probably about half newer destroyers and half "four-pipers" - those built around 1917-18 for World War I duty. The weather on the first trip was rather placid but that was soon to change. As winter approached, the winds got stronger, the waves higher and the air colder. We were ill-prepared for winter in the North Atlantic, and so were all the other naval ships. We had very little cold weather clothing. Luckily, the father of one of the Reservists reporting aboard was a manufacturer of winter coats and our (the DuPont's) small ship service bought a supply of coats from him in Minnesota.

There were usually five destroyers escorting each convoy. A leading destroyer carrying the Convoy Commander up front, then four destroyers at approximately each corner. The convoys speed was determined by the speed of the slowest merchantman; this speed was usually about ten knots, plus or minus a knot. This was slow for us; our standard speed was fifteen knots and flank speed was twenty seven knots. We didn't have Radar at this time so we had to maintain our bearing and distance visually and this could be tricky in rough weather. I remember one return trip, we ran into a very severe storm. We were pitching badly and rolling worse - about 65 degrees maximum as recorded on the inclinometer - and all people standing topside watches were soon soaking wet from the bow spray and rain and frozen to the bone. (Under those conditions, your foul weather clothing would be frozen so stiff that you would have to stand up in the warm wardroom for fifteen to twenty minutes for your clothing to thaw out enough to take it off). After a few days of this miserable weather, it got even worse. One of the destroyers lost her mast due to the violent rolling. We [on the*Dupont*] were patrolling on the starboard bow of the convoy; we were maintaining visual contact with the ship in the convoy closest to us even though it was very foggy and we could see little else. When daylight came and the fog lifted, we discovered that we were the only two ships to be seen - all the other ships were gone. Orders came soon to disband the convoy and proceed independently.

Another westbound trip found us patrolling on the port quarter of a convoy with the *USS Salinas* , a fleet oilier, as the lone American ship on the port quarter corner of the convoy. I believe this was in late October; about the same time as the *Kearney* torpedoing. Shortly before dawn, three German torpedoes hit the convoy. The *Salinas* stopped and we were ordered to stay with her. She had been hit by three torpedoes. But as they had hit in her fuel tanks which were full of water for ballast as she was returning empty... empty of oil. So no-one was hurt and the damage only slowed her a little. And we both soon rejoined the convoy. While the *Salinas* was dead in the water, a sailor ran from amidship up to the bridge yelling that he had seen a periscope. He probably did but we on the bridge didn't see anything— nevertheless, we ran around dropping lots of depth charges. I'm sure we didn't hurt the German submarine, but we surely must have scared him.

I did see the *Kearney* after her torpedoing. She had been tied up to a pier in Reykjavik for a couple of days when we got there. She had been hit in the #1 or #2 fire-rooms and it was sure a mess.

The only connection I had with the *Reuben James* (sunk by German torpedoes in late October) was a personal one. Ensign Craig Spowers and I were good friends as well as being classmates and it was only by a particular quirk of fortune that Craig was assigned to the *Reuben James* and I went to the *DuPont* after graduating from USNA. Craig went down with the *Reuben James*.

This is what happened when the *DuPont* had a collision. We were on escort duty on the port bow of a large eastward bound convoy. Lt (jg) Davey Kellogg was ODD on the mid watch (midnight to four), seas normal, visibility normal. Davey lost sight of the convoy and figured that he had fallen back so he speeded up. He still couldn't see the convoy so he figured that he must be to the left of the convoy so he turned right to get to the convoy. He still couldn't see the convoy and figured that by speeding up, he had got ahead of the convoy. He turned right again to bring him back to position. With this final turn, *DuPont* was actually directly ahead of the convoy and was now on a course that was the opposite of the convoy course; i.e. the *DuPont* and the convoy were on a collision course. The next thing Davey knew (about 3 AM) , the *DuPont* was between two of the columns of ships. If he had stayed on that course, he probably would have sailed through the entire convoy, but he tried to turn to get out of the middle of the merchant ships and in doing so hit one of the ships bow on and slid down the length of the ship grinding off about ten or fifteen feet of our bow. All the ships lights were turned on and we got out of the middle of the convoy somehow. We were ordered back to the Boston Navy Yard and after shoring up the forward bulkheads we proceeded back at about four knots arriving there in early December. In

T.S. Roderick.

Boston, we had a new bow put on, a boiler room removed and a fuel tank added in its place to increase our range and got our first Radar installed. We were returned to duty about the end of December 1941.

Pearl Harbor was bombed while we were in the Boston Navy Yard. When we were repaired, we went to Argentia in early January to start our next convoy run. A call had just come out for my class to volunteer for submarine duty and that very night I took my physical and volunteered for submarine duty in the South Pacific."

Ted was sent to New London, Conn. to a submarine school for three months and was then assigned to the submarine *USS Stingray*. During his 15 months on assignment with the *Stingray*, Ted went on five patrols, each of which lasted about 70 days. Four of the patrols originated from Pearl Harbor and one originated at Brisbane, Australia. Their first patrol was about September of 1942 and went to the Bougainville area of the Solomon Islands, while the Marines were fighting on Guadalcanal. Ted said they sank a number of Japanese supply ships while on that patrol and were subjected to several attacks from depth charges. Damage from depth charges included a broken porcelain toilet bowl (later toilets were made of stainless steel), numerous light bulbs and valves broken, TDC (torpedo data computer) knocked out electrically. Ted said they also had several bombs dropped from air craft on them, and the worst one was dropped while they were making an approach on a large force of warships. It was close enough to break their periscope, making it necessary for the sub to go to Brisbane to wait for a new periscope to be flown in.

On one patrol they laid mines along the China coast, which was a Japanese supply route. They later learned that their mines had sunk a number of enemy ships in that region.

In early 1944 the *Stingray* returned to San Francisco for overhaul. At that time Ted was sent to Pearl Harbor to start a submarine school for enlisted ratings. After about six months he was sent to Portsmouth, N. H. where a new submarine was being constructed. About the time the submarine was completed, Ted got sick and he was later transferred to a school boat at New London, Conn. where he remained for about a year. With the ending of the war, Ted was sent to Pearl Harbor to return to the states with a submarine due for overhaul.

In 1946, after the war had ended, testing of atomic bombs continued. Ted went to the Bikini atoll on the Battleship *Arkansas* for some additional tests. Ted was there when the 4th atomic bomb was tested. It was an air drop over a large number of assembled ships, with the explosion taking place at a low altitude. A few ships were sunk and there was considerable damage to other ships. The 5th atomic bomb test was an under water explosion, which sank a large number of ships including the Battleship *Arkansas*.

Ted remained in the Navy for about 3 years after the war ended and reached the rank of Lt. Commander.

What an unusual military career. From the frigid waters of the North Atlantic on the deck of a destroyer, dropping depth charges on enemy submarines, to being in a submarine on the bottom of the South Pacific, and being the recipient of depth charges launched by the enemy. I am sure it is impossible for those of us who have never been there, to even remotely imagine the terror of having depth charges going off around you, and sitting there on the ocean floor with no air conditioning, wondering if you will survive the attack. My hat is off to those brave men who fought our underwater battles.

A SPECIAL MEMORY

Starting on Dec. 7, 1941 and for the next four years, it was a difficult period in the history of this country. Students of the future will learn how the Japanese struck Pearl Harbor on that fateful morning, beginning World War 11 for the United States.

That date in history now seems so long ago and yet I have many memories of that period of time. Women came out of their homes to work in factories and defense plants, others joined the WAC's or WAVE's. Certain things were rationed, such as sugar and gasoline. Many other things were in short supply or not available at all.

There was fear that the Japanese would strike the west coast. Blackouts were common and factory roofs were painted blue to look like water, as a precaution against bombers. German submarines were along our east coast in great numbers and sank many tankers and other ships along our shores.

Practically every young man was either drafted into military service or enlisted. Almost every kid I knew as a child, every neighbor, every school chum, was in the military during that period of time.

Training camps sprang up all over the country and kids were sent to places they had never heard of before.

Nearly all travel was by train and the trains were packed. Sometimes a military camp would be emptied and troop trains loaded with soldiers would move out every hour headed for a new destination, and very often to a port.

Young men were sent all over the world to do what they had been trained to do. Many were killed in training or in combat later on, and others led charmed lives and returned home with enviable records of distinguished service.

I have no way of' knowing how many of my friends did not make it back but this article is in memory of all those kids I knew who served this country so well during her time of need, and a special memory for those who did not survive..

THE AIR FORCE SERVICE SQUADRON

Jim Ledbetter.

Jim Ledbetter is an old friend from childhood days. He was selected for the draft on October 18, 1941, two months before war was declared on Japan. He was inducted at Ft. Oglethorpe, Ca. and joined the Air Force for three years.

On October 24th, Jim Ledbetter was sent to Kessler Field, Mississippi awaiting assignment. On February 9, 1942 he was sent to Chanute Field to a Parachute Rigging School. Two weeks later he was moved to Shaw Field, S. C. where he packed parachutes. In August he was moved to Fort Dix, N. J. and assigned to the 68th Service Squadron for overseas duty.

On August 6, 1942 Jim sailed from Brooklyn on the *SS Monterey*. Stops were made in Nova Scotia, Scotland, Ireland, and finally Northern England near Hull. At this location they were able to have land quarters in a British barracks. There was some uncertainty as to where they would be staying so their ship just moved from place to place. They were allowed off board at these stops but their quarters were on the ship. They remained in England for over two months and then moved back to Glasgow, Scotland where they remained for one week before sailing for destination unknown on November 14, 1942.

While going through the Strait of Gibraltar, German submarines hit a number of ships in the convoy. His ship was in the middle of the convoy and was not hit. He did not know how many of the ships actually went down.

They arrived in Oran, N. Africa on November 21, 1942, several days after the invasion when 850 allied ships arrived at several ports in Morocco and Algeria. American soldiers swarmed ashore at Casablanca, Oran and Algiers. Three days after arriving in N. Africa, Jim was on a train heading East and arrived in Maison Blanche (near Algiers). He remained in Maison Blanche for about a month and left there on January 4, 1943, destination unknown. He arrived Thelepte, Tunisia on January 9, 1943 and they were only 15 miles from Kasserine Pass. At this location they were subjected to air raids about twenty times daily by German planes. They had no tents but lived in fox holes dug out of the ground. Jim's responsibility was to pack parachutes for the pilots. A Major, flying one of the P-40 fighter planes was shot down by the Germans. When he baled out, his parachute failed to open and of course he was killed. An investigation was held, with Jim called in as the parachute packer. It developed that the parachute had been hit by flak and the heat from the flak had fused the silk material together, causing the parachute to not open. Jim said parachutes were repacked every nine days.

On February 17, 1943 the Germans pushed the U. S. forces out of Kasserine Pass. Another Service Squadron located 25 miles away lost 95%, of their personnel . Jim's outfit of 220 had no casualties. They received advanced warning to leave immediately and burn anything they could not carry. They destroyed a great deal of equipment, including 34 P-40 fighter planes.

The American 1st Armored Division and the U.S. 168th Infantry Regiment emerged from one defensive battle in shape to fight another. They had been brought through Kasserine Pass and Tebessa to the mountains near El Mael Abiod, west of Kasserine Pass. Jim's service squadron was just south of the Pass and when the squadron fled the area, they moved south in Tunisia about 70 miles and there they were able to set up tents for the first time. During the next several months the service squadron moved east and then north to Tunis and then to Bizerte. The British took Tunis on May 7th, the same day the Americans took Bizerte. By May 12th all resistance in Tunisia had ended and the Allies held 252,000 prisoners. Sometimes the group worked with P-38 and P-40 fighter planes and sometimes with the B-

24 four-engine bombers which flew long range missions. Jim said sometimes there would be planes missing when others returned but he had no knowledge of how many planes were lost.

The squadron eventually moved on to Bone, Algeria, and from there to Sicily, which had been taken in fighting there between July 10th and August 17th. By October 9, 1943 they landed at Bari, Italy following initial landings in Italy on September 3rd. From Bari the squadron moved to Foggia for a time and then joined the 557th Service Squadron at Chernoglia. At this location they serviced the B-24's out of a wheat field, with the British on one side of the field and the Americans on the other side.

Jim was in Italy from October of 1943 until January of 1945 when he returned to the United States on rotation. He arrived Fort McPherson, Ga. and was allowed to go home. He reported back to Fort McPherson and was shipped out to Italy again on April 23, 1945. Jim was stationed in Naples for about six months and had no assignment. The war ended and in October of 1945 he returned to the States. Jim was discharged in Indiana on October 13, 1945 with rank of Sergeant.

Jim told me that the most memorable time in his service career was when they were stationed near the Kasserine Pass in Tunisia, living in fox holes, receiving air raids several times a day, and their hurried departure from that location.

B-24 on Flight from Maxwell Field, Alabama.

THE MARINE

John Funk and I have been friends for several years and often play golf together. He grew up in Buffalo, N. Y. and enlisted in the Marines in Feb. of 1942, only two months after the Japanese bombed Pearl Harbor.

John had four close chums and they did many things together. One evening, John announced to his buddies that he had decided to join the Army Air Corps. The five of them discussed the war and how the Marines would be playing such a great part, and the five of them decided they would join the Marines together. The group went down to enlist and John was the only one to pass the required tests. When John boarded the train to leave, his buddies, who had talked him into joining the Marines, were there to wave goodbye. Later on, three of his pals joined the Air Corps and one finally got in the Marines.

John went to Parris Island, S. C. for boot training and was then sent to Quantico, Va. while the Marines decided where to send him. He was then sent to Jacksonville, Fla. to a machinist mate school for twelve weeks. Just before completion of the school , John's mother wrote the Commanding Officer and told him that John had not been home since he enlisted, and it would be nice if he could come home on leave upon graduation from this phase of training. A short time later the school was completed and 53 men were given leave to go home. Two were sent direct to the Mojave Desert in California and one of those was John. John laughs about the incident today but he feels pretty sure that his mother's letter resulted in his banishment to the desert.

There was a Naval Air Station in the desert and John remained there for almost two years, and it turned out to be rather good duty. He was head bartender of the officer's club.

In 1943, John was sent with Marine Air Group 12 to the South Pacific where he was stationed on Emiru Island in the Bismarck Arch. The air group was there to neutralize a nearby island occupied by the Japanese. John was a Leading Chief for a time and then Commander of the Guard,

In late October of 1944 the Marines invaded the Philippines at Leyte. John was with the air group that moved in a short time later. From there they moved on to Mindoro, and later to Mindanao. At one location, John told how he and a group of Marines got loaded on Philippine homemade liquor, which he called "kick-a-poo joy juice".

John said after Mindanao airfield had been secured, a few of the Marines decided they would go for a swim in the surf at Zambo-Ango. They were swimming around in the surf, in the buff, and having a great time when a Zero (Japanese fighter plane) flew over and strafed the group about three times. John said you never saw so many bare bottoms as the marines dived under the water. Fortunately, no one was hit by the bullets.

John's air group went on to China after the Philippine operation and he returned to Cherry Point, N.C. The war ended about that time and John was placed in charge of the separation center. John was discharged in September of 1945 as a Master Sergeant.

John later joined the Marine Reserve and was called back to active duty in 1950 and sent to Korea as First Sergeant Headquarters Company, 1st Engineer Battalion.

John later served one tour in Vietnam as NCO in charge of the Combat Information Bureau (CIB). He retired as a Master Gunnery Sergeant in 1966 after 22 years as a Marine, with service during three wars in the service of his country.

ERNIE PYLE, WAR CORRESPONDENT

In 1935, when I was 15 years of age, the old Chattanooga News started running a daily column called Traveling. It was written by an unknown writer who worked for Scripps-Howard. The articles were distributed to 24 papers that were owned by Scripps-Howard and they were written by Ernie Pyle. Pyle was 35 years of age at that time and he and his wife traveled around the country writing articles on different subjects.

I was really fascinated by the simple and poetic style of this young writer and his stories. I clipped his article from the paper each day an saved them in a folder. This collection of articles has been stored in my trunk for over 60 years. Little did I realize at that time that Ernie Pyle would become one of the most famous war correspondents of all time.

I left Chattanooga in 1939, and sort of lost touch with his daily articles for a brief time. The following year, I read that he had been sent to England to cover the Battle of Britain, I picked up the paper one morning and there was large picture of Ernie Pyle and a two inch headline that screamed; "Pyle watches London Burn from Balcony". That day, Ernie Pyle was introduced to the world. That first dispatch from London was dated December 30, 1940, the beginning of which is quoted here:

"Someday, when peace has returned to this odd world, I want to come to London again and stand on a certain balcony on a moonlit night and look down upon the peaceful silver curve of the Thames with its dark bridges. And standing there, I want to tell somebody who has never seen it how London looked on a certain night in the holiday season of the year 1940. For on that night this old, old city—even thought I must bite my tongue in shame for saying it—was the most beautiful sight I have ever seen. It was a night when London was ringed and stabbed with fire."

Then he went on to picture the destruction he saw by creating a beautiful

Ernie Pyle. National Archives Photo.

Ernie Pyle and tank crew. National Archives Photo.

picture in words, put together as only he could do. Ernie lived and wrote about the war from the muddy roads, the fox holes, the trenches, just like the foot soldiers who lived and died there. He covered the war in North Africa, Sicily, Italy, and France until November of 1944. He later went to the South Pacific in January of 1945. On April 18, 1945 at age 45, Ernie Pyle was shot and killed by a Japanese sniper on the island of Ie Shima, a small island west of Okinawa.

Although I have always been an avid reader and enjoyed the works of many fine writers, I always considered Ernie Pyle my most favorite writer of all time. I am glad I found him in my teen years, when he was unknown, and was able to follow his work while he became the most famous correspondent ever known. A United States stamp was later issued in his honor.

THE SGT MAJOR

Francis Logan was born in Philadelphia, Pa. His friends all call him Frank. When I asked Frank to share his World War II memories, he responded with the following:

"1939 was not a year that I could consider lucrative. What to do when even door to door sales failed. I'll join the Navy. After all there has got to be a war and I will be in on the ground floor. Silly boy.

On October 26, 1939, I reported to the recruit center and was welcomed, not to the Navy or the Marines but to the Air Force. Glamour is what I thought it would be till they said "You, you and you get on that bus." That, of course, was after the oath had been administered.

I was off to Fort Slocum, N.Y. It was an island similar to Alcatraz. Completely surrounded by water. I found the meaning of "KP and "On the double" and that other command "ATTENTION". I learned when to salute, how to be first in the "chow line" and what a latrine was.

The heraldry of the "Pass in review" was a favorite of mine. I was a spit and polish soldier. Since I could two-finger type I was selected to cut up tomatoes but every recruit did that. After I typed something called "Morning Report" which meant that this electrician was given the "MOS" (Military Occupational Specialty) of Company Clerk.

We left Fort Slocum about 15 December 1939 and arrived at the Brooklyn Navy Yard that evening. More physicals prior to boarding the USAT St. Mahiel. During indoctrination we were given a choice of Hawaii or the Panama Canal Zone. Now that was for me. My old boss, Mr. Leslie Griscom, had worked on the Canal locks in his younger years. I liked the guy and sought to follow in his footsteps. Hence, 24 days later I went through that great project. I watched the water being pumped from Gatune Lake into one side of the great lock doors and out the other side and that huge ship rose up and over the hills of the isthmus. I made several trips through the interior of the boiler rooms and pump houses. There were three of everything to allow for maintenance and equipment failures.

My introduction to the Panamanian life style did not happen till after our 90 day restriction to post to be checked inside, outside, topside and bottom side. With shaved head and every part of my body examined very closely we were given liberty (the only word that had it's origin in the Navy) to visit the old city of Christobal. From my Catholic upbringing it was a shock to be grabbed at by prostitutes half my age.

I was assigned as assist to the crew chief on a P-28. A Mono-wing fighter (I use the term "fighter" very loosely) made of wooden wings with a fabric stretched tight and painted a brilliant blue and yellow, the Army Air Corps colors. It was one of my jobs to clean that plane. You could only walk on the wings. The walkway on the left side of the craft was reinforced with plywood so the pilot had access to the cockpit. The only armament was a 30 cal. machine gun that had to be synchronized with the propeller of the aircraft. A pilot could possibly shoot himself down if the prop got hit. I never saw that happen but I understand it did happen during ground tests.

Every day one of the tow motors with a flatbed trailer would come from the mess hall with our coffee and cake. This was a time for meeting my coworkers. The First Sgt. complimented me on the work I had done and asked if I was interested in making some money as a postal clerk. It didn't take a bomb to fall on me, I took the job, a regular U.S. Post office position. The mail had to be sorted both going out and coming in. We were kept very busy but that was all the duty we had. We could leave the base when we were not on duty. Joe Stallings was a red headed rebel and Johnny Robinson was a born and raised New England guy. The Postmaster was a nice guy. His name was Moses De La Pena of Panamanian descent. In Spanish it meant "Moses, of the rock".

I was approached by Master Sgt. Collins for a job as security clerk and had to take an oath before some bigshots that I would not reveal anything that I read or heard while in the performance of my duties.

I had to read letters going out and coming in to check for subversive content. I only found one Major who seemed kinda funny to me. His magazines and letters were full of red underlines and circled sentences. It turned out he was a relative of a Congressman and had a business in the states and was no more a spy than I was.

Some of the GI's tried to create a code to let their families know where they were. My family knew I was in Panama because I was down there long before the restrictions started. Besides that, anyone interested could ask any prostitute and they could tell you any information that was available. Troop units and T.0's (Table of organization's) were known by everyone. Every effort was made to suppress information but to no avail.

When we first arrived at Albrook Field on the Pacific side of the isthmus and-the south side of the canal, we were quartered in aircraft hangars but after the barracks were completed we moved in as "permanent party".

San Blas Indians served as waiters at every meal. When a serving dish was down to one last spoonful it was held aloft and these little barefoot Indians would run to take the empty while another would bring a full one.

11:00 AM to 1:00 PM was designated as quiet hour. You could hear a pin drop. Some guys would read or write letters while others decided to nap. If that was not your thing to do you could go out in the hot sun and jog or lift weights or swim in the base pool but I liked to play tennis and I thought I did it well. All of a sudden all that activity stopped. Gone were the little Indians and the meals were cafeteria style. Everything was a lineup.

The only thing we still had an abundance of was showers and with the hot weather the water ran most of the time except when the latrine orderlies had their job to do.

Troops were shifted all over the Isthmus and we were designated a training base. There were plane loads of fledgling pilots that to me at an old age of 22 seemed like babies, but they would come in, be assigned, and 30 days later sent on to another training facility. These young people would write letters by the score and I had to either cut out a lot of what was said or, it was too bad, turn it over to my Colonel. One of our "outposts" for skip bombing training was in Rio Hato R de P. I was sent as part of the Headquarters Squadron and on December 7, 1941 I was at my desk writing a letter home when my radio announced the bombing of Pearl Harbor.

For some reason the next 48 hours were filled with all kinds of trucks and barrack bags and soldiers from every branch of service. In two weeks there were over 200,000 men moved to Europe and to the Pacific. We knew then that the Pacific Theatre of operations was being passed over in favor of the European Theatre because England was being threatened by an invasion by the Axis.

It seemed almost simultaneous that we started to receive P-36 fighter aircraft and a few B-18 bombers. Since we were a fighter base the bombers were sent to the newly constructed Howard Field on the north side of the Canal. Day and night the aircraft flew training missions and protected the bombers on runs out to sea to hunt for submarines that were sinking our ships. Once in a while we would lose a plane and a pilot and on occasion a bomber would end in-the drink. When dealing with munitions there has to be accidents and so it was with us. I had to "pull" guard duty. On one occasion a frog in the armament section croaked while sitting on an unbalanced piece of metal. All hell broke loose when the guard reported it to me. I called the O.D. (Officer of the day) and we had about 50 men around that armament shack. We had a good laugh when the truth was known.

I had made friends with a few of the young pilots and eventually they all left for combat. I still hear from two of them but they are both very sick men.

After the Rio Hato sojourn, I went back to Albrook Field and then to France Field on the Atlantic and from there to the Galapagos Islands. That was a place to remember. It was called "The Rock". Formed from an earlier volcanic explosion and covered with at least a foot of volcanic dust, no one was ever clean. Our "Johns" had to be drilled and blasted out of the rock and the outhouse placed on top. We had gotten some pretty lousy meals and diarrhea was rampant. The engineers worked day and night building new toilet facilities till the siege was over.

It was while I was on "The Rock" that our first B-24's were delivered. We called them pregnant cows, but they were the best workhorse at the beginning of the war.

Later on, early in 1942, we saw our first super-fortress. A crew of 12 manned the huge sleek machine. There were machine gun turrets on top, in the tail, in the belly and both port and starboard waist areas. When they were being loaded with bombs and torpedoes, we clerical people were amazed at the number of explosives that were put aboard.

Their "search and destroy" missions carried them from the Galapagos all over the Caribbean Sea and several thousand square miles of the Pacific Ocean. Once in a while one of the crew would get sick or something and we would get a chance to go out on a "sea hunt". Rank had its privileges. Master

Sergeants went first after the "BRASS" but it would only be the administrative "BRASS". Combat officers tried to stay down once in a while even though they did like their job.

When I returned to the Canal Zone I was put on the I.G. (Inspector General) team and traveled all over the 4th Air Force bases. Caracus, Venezula, Talara, Peru and Bogata, Columbia. We also inspected the Virgin Islands and that miriad of bases. I even got to Washington D.C. when a General hitched a ride. Boy! Could that guy drink. His name does not belong in this story.

I bounced from place to place after the Germans surrendered. Then came the three R's: Rehabilitation, Recuperation and Recovery. Shortened to the point system. According to your time of enlistment, rank, number of dependents and your age, you received credits toward state-side rotation. I don't remember how many points I had but I think it was 24 and that put me in the first wave.

I boarded a plane and flew to Amarillo, Texas. Then the darndest, hottest train ride I ever had to Fresno, Calif. for a few days and then to San Francisco and 30 days of leave back home.

When I returned to San Francisco, I was assigned as Sgt. Major of the 4th Air Force. My Adjutant was a Major, a former mail man, but a very industrious older gent. The Executive Officer was a real giant of a man. The two-star General was a brilliant man but as gentle as a lamb. I had two WAC secretaries.

My wife and son came out and we took a "share" apartment near Golden Gate Park. The share apartment did not work out too well and we left. My next move was to Salinas, Calif., the lettuce center of the world.

After Salinas we were moved to an air base in far southern Calif., and from that point to Fort Dix, N. J. where I received my "ruptured duck" and my discharge papers.

There are a lot of stories that go with that tour of duty. The most amusing was the night the cow was shot dead during an alert. The private, I hope he remembers, thought the Germans had landed in Rio Hato and seeing a shadow decided to fire on it. I was watch sergeant and I went fast in my jeep with the O.D. close behind and with that many flashlights we found our "intruder" dead as a doornail. The Panamanian farmer was happy because he got paid more for that cow than he ever saw in his life.

In another incident, one of our early P-28's was up on a training mission and, against orders, dived on an alligator swamp. The pilot never pulled out of his dive and was killed. I volunteered to go on the search and rescue mission. It was on foot and through dense underbrush and the San Blas Indians hacked a path with bolos till they came to what seemed like a wall of saplings. They were entwined with vines as we later found out, impenetrable with the bolos. We had to skirt over two miles around that thicket and finally found an access we could get through. The other side of that thicket was marshland and full of snakes and alligators. Thousands of snakes and ugly, vicious gators. Later that swamp was fire bombed and became part of a four-lane highway on the north side of the Panama Canal from Howard Field on the Pacific side to France Field on the Atlantic. The highway was completed in record time of 4 months and 3 days, a distance of about 50 miles."

THE 75TH INFANTRY DIVISION

Billy Phillips is a member of our Virginia Beach Seniors golf group. He was born in Hampton, Va. and was drafted in November of 1942. He was inducted into the service at Petersburg, Va.

Billy was sent to Ft. Fisher, N. C., near Wilmington, for anti-aircraft training. From there, he was sent to Camp Polk, La. as part of the cadre for the new 75th Infantry Division. Then he was sent to Camp Breckenridge, Ky. for infantry training. After extensive training, Billy and the 75th Division moved to New York on the next phase of their mission. They shipped out on the army transport *Edmund B. Alexander* on Oct. 22, 1944. It had been only three months since the Allies invaded France on June 6th and Billy knew they were headed into battle to do the things they had been trained to do.

The 75th Division arrived Swansea, Wales on November 2, 1944. The troops were scattered throughout the area but Billy remembers being in a schoolhouse. Most of the men were later moved by rail to Southampton, England.

The 75th then crossed the English Channel and disembarked at LeHavre, France on Dec. 13, 1944. Three days later, on Dec. l6th, the Germans surprised the First Army's Belgian defenses with a counter offensive which opened a gap 60 miles wide and drove a wedge 50 miles deep into the American lines. The Americans held firm on the German flanks, however.

The 75th was diverted from their intended mission and on Dec. 19th left France by motor and rail to take its place in the action against the Germans in the Belgian Bulge. They arrived Bilsen, Belgium on December 21st. and defensive positions were taken up near Tohogne, Belgium. They engaged the enemy at several locations but the freezing weather and deep snow was very difficult on the troops. Frost bite and trench foot cases increased in large numbers as days went by.

Billy was part of the Pioneer Squadron, responsible for demolition, mine sweeping, ammunition supply to the rifle companies, etc.

The First Battalion suffered its first casualties on Dec. 29th near Manhay, and I Company's first casualties occurred on Jan. 1, 1945 in Manhay. On Jan. 5th, the regiment pulled back for three days of rest in Creppe-Spa, Belgium. On Jan. 9th the regiment marched eleven hours over 22 miles of icy roads and knee deep snow and arrived Basse Bodeux, Belgium at 5AM. On Jan. 15th the 291st Infantry went into its first attack as a regiment. Their objective was the high ground outside Grand Hallaux. Early morning of the 16th, Company I received heavy casualties but reached their objective. The First Battalion on Jan. 17th moved on to Ville de Boil, while 3rd Battalion occupied Petit Thier. On Jan. 20th, Company I moved outside Aldringen. Third Battalion moved to Beck, Belgium. St. Vith was taken on Jan. 24th. B Company suffered heavy casualties in an attack against Aldrigen. After these battles were concluded in sub zero weather and deep snow, the 291st Infantry's mission was completed. The Germans had been pushed back and flattened the Bulge. Later, it was announced that Allied casualties in December on all fronts in western Europe totaled 74, 783. The Battle of the Bulge in January added greatly to these numbers.

The 291st was relieved of their defenses on Jan. 26th and moved by train to the "Colmer Pocket" in France.

It was about this time that Billy was placed on detached duty and sent to Holland to learn how to operate an outboard motor boat. With this assignment completed, Billy returned to the 75th and later engaged in moving troops across the Rhine River.

The 291st Regiment detrained at Frepelle, France on Jan. 28th and went on the offensive on Feb. 1, 1945. Wolfgantzen was the key city to the walled fortress town of Neuf-Brisach, which guarded the last escape bridge over the Rhine. Company I and Second Battalion suffered heavy casualties on Feb. 4th as they pushed their attack. Wolfgantzen was taken on Feb. 5th and the men had a chance to rest. Food and wine were plentiful in the cellars of the city.

On Feb. 15th, with the Germans chased out of Colmer, the 291st Infantry headed for Holland to relieve a British unit in a holding position on the Maas River, and remained until March 1st. Not a great deal of action there but many casualties were suffered from booby traps and mines. On March 7th, the 291st Infantry took up defensive positions on the west bank of the Rhine River south of Wesel. First crossings of the Rhine were made on March 24th. In the final phase of the Ruhr campaign, the 291st took Datteln, Brambauer, Schellenberg, Syburg , Castrop-Rauxel , Kottenburg , Eichl inghofen , Bittermork, Hocksten , Mollen , Dorsten, Ickern, Rutgers and Kirchlinde. Prisoners were taken by the hundreds as the Germans gave up. On April 22nd, the regiment moved to vicinity of Bad Driburg and took over an area of occupation.

The final crack-up in Germany started on May 4th when all the forces in north Germany, the Netherlands and Denmark surrendered to General Montgomery's 12th Army Group. On May 7th, the Germans surrendered unconditionally to the Supreme Allied Command at Rheims, France.

When the war ended, the 75th served on occupation duty for about a month and they were then moved to Southern France to await a ship to carry them to the South Pacific.

With the surrender of the Japanese, Billy was moved to a location outside Paris waiting for a ride back to America. Billy said they were able to go into Paris every night. Their ride finally came and they returned to New Jersey and Billy was discharged in March of 1946. Billy was a PFC.

DISASTER IN THE AIR

It has not been too long ago since the world watched in horror as the space shuttle Challenger exploded in flight killing the seven members of the crew. Millions watched on TV as the terrible tragedy unfolded in vivid color right before their eyes. It was a terrible, terrible accident and one the world will not soon forget.

This accident reminded me of a period in our history when many planes exploded in the air and each had 10 or 12 men on board. It was not viewed on television, but if it had been, the horror would have been as great as the Challenger accident.

On August 1, 1943 179 B-24 bombers took off from North Africa to bomb the oil fields at Ploesti, Romania. Each plane carried a crew of 12. Of the 179 B-24's dispatched on the raid, 11 aborted and 2 others crashed, leaving 166 to attack the target. Of these, 53 failed to return and most of the others were damaged. Some 440 men were killed, many others were wounded, and about 200 became prisoners of war. Many of the planes that were lost blew up in the air when hit by enemy fighters or ground fire.

By this time the United States had accumulated large numbers of B-17 planes in England to strike German forces in Europe. We had not yet learned that bombers without fighter escort could not fly deep into the heart of Germany without extreme danger to planes and crews.

Plans were made to make a concentrated attack on the German aircraft factory at Regensburg and a simultaneous attack on the ball-bearing factories at Schweinfurt. At least 147 B-17's were to attack Regensburg and 230 B-17's were to strike Schweinfurt. The dual raid took place on August 17, 1943 and the bombers took off from England at dawn.

Over Germany these two bomber groups were met by several hundred German fighters and the United States lost 60 B-17's in the two raids. Another

100 bombers were damaged by flak or fighters, and many of these were damaged so badly they had to be destroyed. Some 600 young men lost their lives as planes exploded in the air or crashed in flames. This did not include those dead and dying in the damaged planes that returned.

Two months later, in October, during a one week period the U. S. made similar raids on Bremen, Marienburg, Danzig, Monster and back to Schweinfurt. In that one week, we lost 148 bombers and nearly 1,500 aircrew. Each time a B-17 went down or exploded in flight, 10 young men were lost. These disasters brought a halt to deep-penetration daylight missions over Europe by the U. S. air force until long-range escort fighters became available in 1944.

When I think of the Challenger explosion, I always remember the many times similar things happened during World War II and there was little or no publicity at the time. Notification to the family merely stated "your son was lost over Europe".

Many of my high school friends were lost on missions over Europe during that time.

THE U.S.S. PC 1193

Johnny Nichols was one of the best friends I ever had. He passed away on March 7, 1997. Johnny was born in Georgia and we both were working for the railroad in Cincinnati, Ohio when the Japanese bombed Pearl Harbor on December 7, 1941. Johnny immediately left his job and joined the Navy. Although Johnny and I remained friends for the past 56 years, we rarely ever talked about the war years. After Johnny passed away, his widow dug up some of his war records and sent them to me . Johnny left the following with regard to PC 1193:

"Following a brief stint in two navy schools I was assigned to the precommissioning crew of the PC 1193 as a third class yeoman. This ship was the product of the Consolidated Shipbuilding Corp., Morris Height, N.Y.

Johnny Nichols.

When I arrived on the scene in December 1942 she was tied up on the Bronx side of the Harlem River at about 175th St. The Commanding Officer was Loren H. Kiser, Lt. USN; the Executive Officer, Nathan C. Sutton, Lt. USNR; Communications Officer, Milton W. Nosek, Lt. (jg) USNR.

The ship was Diesel powered, fluid drive, her screws turned inboard, which made her easy to steer, no radar and only about a third of the crew had ever been to sea and I was one of those who had not.

In early February 1943 we sailed out of 'The Narrows' into the teeth of a booming gale, headed for Miami, Fla. About 72 hrs later, in the wee hours of the morning, we saw the dim lights of Hamilton, Bermuda. We had cut speed to reduce pounding and were forced to rig life lines from the bridge to the mess hall. Our trip around Hatteras was made about 600 miles out in the Atlantic. What was normally about a three-day run took us 6 days and upon arrival in Miami we were a sorry mess. Of my 29 months of sea duty in WWII that storm will be with me always .

Upon arrival Lt. Kiser was relieved by N.C. Sutton and Lt. (jg) Nosek took over as Exec.

We were assigned to the Submarine Chaser Training Center, Miami, as a training vessel and for any other duties that might arise.

The German U Boat menace was at its height on our east coast and we were called upon many times to 'make a chase'.

One night about 10:00, we were called out with only the port section aboard (starboard was on liberty). A U Boat was reported surfaced by Great Issac shoal about 60 miles east of Miami. We were a squadron of four, two other PC's and a DE. We were gone 16 days with half a crew, dropped 96 depth charges and upon arrival back in Miami could sleep standing up. A kill was never confirmed

We did convoy and patrol duty as far north as West Palm Beach and as far south and west as Dry Tortugas.

On May 21, 1943 Nathan C. Sutton was relieved as CO by Milton Nosek, now a full Lieut.

On Sept. 10, 1943 Milton Nosek was relieved of command and assigned as Prospective Commanding Officer of the PCE 873 which was being fitted out at the Albina Engine and Machine Works, Inc. in Portland, Ore. He asked me if I would like to be assigned to his new command. I consented and departed the PC 1193 on Sept. 17, 1943 as a second class yeoman.

I never knew what became of the old 1193."

A further search of Johnny's records revealed that in June 1943 the PC 1193, along with several other vessels, attacked a German submarine off the coast of Florida. They kept the submarine down for about 20 hours and finally left the scene, convinced that they had sunk a big, bad German U-boat. In later years it was developed that the German submarine was the U-190.

Several years after the war ended, Elmo Allen, a member of DE-16, one of the ships involved in the submarine chase, provided additional details about the U-190, when he wrote as follows:

"Several years ago I got in touch with a German U-boat sailor who had been captured on the U-234, his ship was enroute to Japan with many of the components for the A-Bomb - Japan was working on the bomb at that time, as was Germany when they surrendered. This German sailor kindly went to the U-Boat archives and looked up some records for the dates I sent him. He also contacted the U-Boat Skipper who remembered the incident only too well. He said it was the most terrifying experience of the entire war.

Another confirmation came about earlier when Lt. Robert Shanklin went aboard a German super-tanker in New Jersey years after the war. The Lt. worked for a large oil company and went aboard on company business. He was invited to the wardroom by the German officers, got into a deep conversation with the Skipper of the tanker. Eventually the conversation turned to World War II. The German said he had been a U-boat Skipper. Mr. Shanklin mentioned having served on a DE. At the mention of a "DE" the German said his most horrible experience of all time came about because of a U.S. Navy 'DE'. One thing led to another and Mr. Shanklin suddenly mentioned the date and approximate location - the German's eyes just about popped out of his head; he got out his charts and pointed to the exact location which Shanklin agreed with. Each excitedly began to relate what went on during those 20 long hours. Mr. Shanklin said, when the conversation was over with, the German poured both of them a very big drink and they looked one another in the eye and shook hands. Looking back I am happy they survived their ordeal although none of us certainly felt that way about it back then. The German passed away very recently"

Additional information on the German submarine U-190 was developed. The U-190, under the command of Max Wintermeyer and executive officer Zur See Hans Edwin Reith, departed the submarine base at Lorient, France, putting out to sea for a 2 1/2 month patrol after repairs and crew leave. The mission of U-190 was to sink Allied shipping off the east coast of the United States. This was May 1, 1943. Shortly after arriving on station in mid-May the U-190 was attacked but escaped unharmed and proceeded on patrol to the south in its search for enemy shipping. On June 12th the U-190 had the encounter with the USS PC 1193 and the other ships involved in the incident.

*PC 1193 coming alongside USS
Edgar G. Chase DE16 1943.*

The German U-190 was pinned down on the bottom for 20 hours during which time many depth charges were dropped. After no sound was detected from the U-boat, the four ships left the area after some of the sailors reported sighting clothing, splinters and other debris floating in the water. It was never known but entirely possible the U-190 ejected this debris through torpedo tubes in an attempt to fool the U.S. ships.

Those 20 hours were to be a lot longer for the crew of U-190 which was sitting on the bottom of the Atlantic - playing a game of cat and mouse with the ships overhead. With their crew ordered to remain totally silent, resting at their battle stations, attempting to conserve the rapidly depleting oxygen supply, no movement allowed for fear that any noise might be detected by the patrolling ships overhead. 12 hours was generally believed to be the maximum endurance of a subs crew under such conditions. Kapitan Wintermeyer was to relate many years later that this was the worst of experiences for both he and his crew during the war. Most of the crew were incapacitated due to lack of oxygen. When the surface ships departed the area most were physically unable to perform their duties and there were scarcely enough able bodied men to get U-190 underway, but they did and lived to fight another day.

The U-190 surrendered to Canadian naval forces on May 13, 1945. On October 21, 1947 U-190 was taken to the site where the U-190 sank *HMCS Esquemalt* with heavy loss of life. U-190 sea valves were opened and U-190 was sunk on that spot.

One of the four ships involved in the incident with the U-190 was later involved with another situation, but I am not sure whether Johnny and the PC 1193 were out on that call. The *USS Edgar G. Chase*-DE-16 was enroute to the scene of a submarine sighting north of Havana. On their way to the scene, they were passed by a blimp also headed for the location. The blimp announced to the crew of the DE-16, on their bull horn, that they would see them there. The blimp was shot down by the submarine, one crewman was killed and the others injured when the blimp's depth charges exploded beneath them after the gondola sank. The survivors were rescued and taken into Havana. The blimp was the K-74 and to my knowledge was the only blimp lost to enemy action in World War II.

THE USS PCE 373

Johnny Nichols left the USS PC 1133 in September of 1943 to join his former skipper, Lt. Nosek, on the USS PCE (Patrol Craft Escort) 873. The PCE 873 was placed in service on December 15, 1943 in Portland, Oregon,

Johnny would stay with the PCE 873 until the end of the war. He learned the true meaning of "Join the Navy and see the world".

During the early weeks of January 1944, the PCE 873 was engaged in their shake down around Terminal Island, San Pedro, California, and at the West Coast Sound School in San Diego.

In early February their shake down was completed and they reported to U. S. Naval Frontier Base, San Diego, for duties as patrol vessel and school ship for trainees of West Coast Sound School. In August the PCE 873 reported to San Pedro for general duty.

On October 6th, Lt. Nosek left the vessel and was replaced by Lt. H. C. Ikenberry, Jr., USNR.

The PCE 873 then spent a couple of months at Terminal Island being converted into a PCE (C) (Patrol Craft Escort, Control).

On January 5, 1945 the 373 left the states and headed for Pearl Harbor and on to the Marshall Islands. Working out to Saipan and then to Ulithi Island as escort command ship, she then began her tour in the active part of the war against Japan. In late February the 873 arrived Hinuangan Bay, Leyte and began training for the invasion of Okinawa. The primary job of the 373 was control - control of the amphibious landings and the eventual supplying of the troops ashore.

The first taste of combat against the enemy was on March 26, 1945. Assuming station off Yakabi Shima, the 873 took part in the initial bombardment of Green Beach Z-2. After controlling the landings of the three initial assault waves, the J73 proceeded to the vicinity of Purple Beach Z-1,

Toyasiki Shima and assisted in further landings. After all landing operations were completed the 373 spent a good deal of time on anti-submarine work around Kerama Retto and in the vicinity of Okinawa Shima. On April 16th, acting in the capacity of control vessel, the 873 took part in the amphibious landings on Ie Shima. On April 25th the 873 was again assigned escort duty and returned to Saipan and remained on patrol duties for a time. In late June the 873 participated in assault landings on Kume Shima, Nansei Shoto. before once again returning to patrol duties.

During the late stages of the war, the 873 was on patrol to Saipan, to San Pedro Bay, Leyte Island, to Subic Bay, Luzon Island,

"Salty"

Philippine Islands. The war ended on August 15, 1945 and a few days later Johnny left for good old home.

The USS PCE (C) was later decommissioned on September 1, 1955 and transferred to the Republic of Korea under the Military Assistance Act.

A TRIBUTE TO OZ

Now and then I read an article about the shortage of heroes and how badly the young People need heroes to look up to. Of course, such articles are referring to national heroes but what about the unsung heroes that are in every neighborhood and every walk of life. We don't really have to look very far to find these man of great dignity and courage, these men who loved their country above all else.

I served in the Naval Air Corps and later the Army Air Corps with a dear friend who passed away in 1985. I wrote a tribute to my friend and it read as follows:

"In one of General McArthur's final speeches he quoted from an old soldier's ballad when he said 'old soldiers never die, they just fade away'. I think there must be some special place in heaven for those brave men who have fought our battles and lived their lives in almost constant danger. When their war days are over and no more battles to be fought, I think it must be true - 'they just fade away'. My World War II buddy, Col. C. R. Osborne, Jr. (called "Bob" by his wife) lived and fought our battles for over 30 years. He was a fighter pilot and a good one. He was shot down twice, survived, and returned from many missions with bullet holes in his plane. Death was often but an inch away and yet he always escaped the violent death that could have been his at any time. A veteran of World War II, the Korean War, the Vietnam War, and the war in Laos - there had been a lot of 'wind down the runway', as Oz often said. His face had a weathered look, attesting to the many hardships he had endured, but his hair was still dark and his eyes still sparkled when last we saw him. He was proud of the service he had rendered his country and his home was lined with books, pictures, certificates, maps of Laos and Vietnam, and the silver wings and medals he had earned during his years of service for the United States and its people. At 1:30 PM on

1985, at Fort Sam Houston in San Antonio, Texas. while the missing man formation flew overhead, the drums rolled as taps was played the last time for Oz as he was laid to rest with full military honors. Hopefully, this country will continue to enjoy the freedom he treasured and which he so valiantly fought to preserve. May he now rest in peace."

So, if you are looking for a hero, you can probably find one in your own neighborhood, someone much like Oz.

C. R. Osborne Jr.

THE P-40 PILOT

My good friend Lyle Boley was raised in Kansas and attended Kansas State University. He was at the age where he had to register for the draft before World War II started. He signed up for pilot training, passed the required tests, and was awaiting call when he was drafted in March of 1941. He was sent to Camp Robinson, Ark. where he remained for two months before being called for pilot training. Because of his ROTC training in college, Lyle was used as one of the instructors while at Camp Robinson.

Lyle was sent to Sikeston, Mo. for primary flight training in the PT-17. From there he was sent to Randolph Field, Tex. for basic pilot training in the PT-13 and PT-15. The next stop was Kelly Field in San Antonio, Tex. where he trained in the AT-6. Lyle received his commission as 2nd Lieutenant on Dec. 12, 1941 upon graduation from flight training. This was just a few days after the Japanese bombed Pearl Harbor.

Lyle was assigned to the Training Command for a short time and served as an instructor for cadets in advanced pilot training. Lyle was then moved to Mitchell Field, N. Y. and assigned to the 8th Pursuit Group. They were told they would be going to Alaska. When it was learned that this group had not received training in the P-40 fighter plane, experienced pilots had to be found for the trip to Alaska. Lyle's group started training in the P-40 and they formed the 51st Fighter Group. This group was formed by the 24th, 25th and 26th Fighter Squadrons. The 24th went to Baltimore, the 25th went to Philadelphia, and the 26th went to Norfolk. Lyle went to Norfolk, Va. with the 26th squadron.

With training completed in Norfolk, the 26th Squadron returned to Mitchell Field in New York and joined the other two squadrons. Their planes were loaded on the aircraft carrier *USS Ranger* and the Pilots moved on board. They departed, destination unknown.

Lyle Boley and wife.

The carrier stopped at the Ascension Islands for refueling and a little relaxation for the men. From there they moved to the Gold Coast of West Africa. At that location the 72 pilots flew their P-40's off the carrier deck. Lyle said this was the first time army aircraft had ever flown off of a carrier (of course no catapult). The pilots had done a little short take-off practice in New York but the runways were quite a bit longer than the 430 feet allotted on the carrier. What an exciting first time for the men who took off from the carrier!

The group flew to Accra, West Africa for their first stop. From there they leap-frogged across Africa and Egypt and on to India. They were able to see the pyramids, the sphinx, on the way through Egypt, and the Taj Mahal in India.

The planes stopped in Karachi, India where they trained for a short time, and then moved to northeast India near Burma. At this location DC-3's and other cargo planes would load and fly supplies into China. It was the job of the P-40 fighter group to provide protection for these supply flights. The group also took turns patrolling their base at 20,000 feet to prevent any surprise attacks from the Japanese. This was about August of 1942.

Prior to the arrival of this fighter group, supplies into China were moved by land over the Burma Road. Gasoline and oil were moved over this route for the Chinese air force, as well as other supplies. Lt. General Joseph Stilwell was chief of staff to Generalissimo Chiang Kai-shek and was in command of the Chinese Fifth and Sixth Armies, operating with the British in Burma. On April 19, 1942 a Japanese force estimated at 100,000 men, with tank and aerial support, began a new thrust into Burma. General Stilwell later said his forces took a "hell of a beating". His march out of Burma into India started on May 1, 1942 and ended May 20th, after a 140 mile trek through the

Burmese jungles. With the loss of the Burma Road to the Japanese, it was then necessary to fly supplies over Burma into China. This accounted for the P-40's being sent to India to provide coverage for the cargo planes flying from India into China.

The air group eventually arranged a way to carry three 20 lb. bombs under each wing and a 500 lb. bomb in the belly of the plane. Bombing runs were then made on selected targets in Burma. On one trip across Burma, it was learned the Japanese had set up a command post along the Burma Road. Lyle remembers dropping one of his 20 lb. fragmentation bombs and saw it hit and skid into the structure with complete destruction.

On another flight Lyle became separated from his group and came upon a group of twin engine Japanese bombers, called "Betty's". Lyle shot down the rear bomber in the group and then noticed four Zero fighter planes headed his way. He turned his P-40 and got out of there as fast as possible.

The range of the P-40 was about one hour and forty minutes when at full throttle. In July of 1942, the 25th Fighter Squadron in India was moved into China to replace the Flying Tigers.

General Hap Arnold visited the pilots in India on one occasion and most of the men were reluctant to talk to the top brass. Lyle offered to talk with the General and responded to his questions about how many hours the planes had flown and other matters. The General also inquired about the rank of the pilots and Lyle told him the men had not received any promotions since graduating from flight school. General Arnold left and two days later each member of the fighter group was promoted to 1st Lieutenant.

Lyle flew 39 missions while in India and after 19 months he returned to the states in November of 1943 as a 1st Lieutenant.

While on a visit home Lyle had a return of malaria and spent some time in the Veterans Hospital in Topeka, Kansas. Then he was sent to Santa Monica, Calif. to a redistribution station. On January 10, 1944, Lyle was sent back to his home with a stop in Salt Lake City for assignment. His orders called for him to report to Baton Rouge. Enroute, Lyle stopped off in Norfolk, Va. and was married on February 14, 1944.

At his new location in Baton Rouge, Lyle was back in the Training Command and served as Asst. Operations Officer. Lyle remained there for several months and was promoted to Captain.

Lyle was then sent to Waco, Texas, for about three months and the war in Europe ended on May 7, 1945. He was then given an opportunity to get out of the service. Lyle was sent to Ft. Levinsworth, Kansas where he received his discharge in June of 1945.

Lyle remained in the Reserve and advanced to the rank of Major before completing his service with 20 years and 3 months.

MY LITTLE RED HEAD

I was a newspaper carrier during my high school years. When I graduated in 1937 the local paper made me a District Manager in their circulation department. I was placed in charge of the newspaper carriers in one of the suburbs of Chattanooga, Tenn. It was my responsibility to see that the carriers delivered their papers on time, paid for them on a weekly basis, and worked to increase the number of customers on their route.

One day a little red-headed boy came to me and wanted to become a paper boy. He had more freckles on his face that I had ever seen and his hair was a brilliant red, sort of brick red. His name was Lawrence and he was 13 years old. I knew he could use the money, so I gave him the first paper route that came open.

He was sort of a misfit in a group of pretty nice boys. He was a prankster and always noisy at our meetings, and I always worried that he might not pay for his papers at the end of the week.

I worked with Lawrence patiently and I began to see him grow. He respected me and I really think he would have done anything to help me, and I did many things to try and help him.

I left the Chattanooga News in January of 1939 and still, I often thought

Lawrence S. Medlin.

of that little red head who had become such a part of my life for over a year. His was the only face I remembered among the boys who worked for me.

Five years later during the war, I picked up a Chattanooga paper one day and there was a picture of my little red head. What a fine looking young man he had turned out to be. But, he was dead at age 19, killed in a plane crash while serving his country. He was a gunner and had advanced to the position of Staff Sgt.

I never forgot that eager little boy who looked out from behind those freckles but never lived to realize his dreams.

OPERATION STARVATION

My good golfing friend Francis McCarthy was born in Massachusetts and enlisted in the Navy in Boston on December 15, 1942. He was sent home to await further orders and was called to active duty in January of 1943.

Francis was sent to Great Lakes Training Center for recruit training. In April of 1943 he was sent to Moffett Field in California for further training. At this location Francis earned the rank of Seaman Second Class after completion of the required study courses.

Francis was then transferred to Hawthorne, Nevada where he remained from June 1943 to November 1943. His assignment there was working in the ammunition depot loading and unloading ammunition. He was made Seaman First Class and awaited orders for overseas duty.

Between November 1943 and January 1944 Francis received commando training and was sent to San Bruno, California to await transportation His group was finally loaded aboard a transport which ended up in Guam. There they waited for supplies and then moved on to Tinian, an island in the Mariannas. This was about a ten hour trip on an LST. Francis said his group consisted of about 50 men and officers. He said there were no natives on this island. The group initially lived at the Naval Air Station depot.

The next task was to unload the LST and set up their station overlooking the air station and the bay between Saipan and Tinian. Francis said the hill where they were located was very steep and he remembered one truck on which the load shifted to the rear and the front end of the truck stood up and rested on the rear body. The group helped the Seabees in erecting the Quonset huts and other buildings and finally their sleeping quarters.

Francis said it was very hot and he remembers cutting down their dungarees to shorts while cutting a hole in the road to run a pipe to get water from the water tank to their buildings.

Francis said their camp consisted of two Quonset huts 40 x 200 feet for assembly and testing of mines, one mess hall, about ten huts for barracks, one hut for administration, and one for sick bay. Their ready revetment, where mines were stored, was located about 800 yards away and 90 feet down the hill below their camp. On one occasion, the hobnail shoes worn by the Seabees caused an explosion while the Seabees were putting canvas covers over the mines. Several mines were lost as were several trucks, and a number of men were injured. The Seabees were then assigned shoes with rubber soles. It was later discovered that three revetments in the lower storage had exploded.

When the group got into full operation, they started a progressive program to inspect, reassemble, test and final closure of the mines. Francis had the job to install the detonator into the extender. There were only two assembly points and Francis installed half of all the detonators that went into the "Operation Starvation" of Japan program.

The mines assembled at Tinian were taken by B-29 planes and dropped by parachute in the waters around Japan at strategic locations. These were 2000 pound mines which were floated in by parachute and dropped to the ocean floor. Some of the mines were magnetic, some were pressure mines, and others responded to acoustic noise. The program was designed to help disrupt the shipment of food supplies into Japan.

Francis was still at Tinian when the war ended and he returned to the states in 1945. He arrived in San Diego with the rank of AN2, Mine Man Second Class. Francis stayed in the U.S. Navy until 1962 and retired with the rank of MNCS, a Senior Chief in mine warfare.

A FOUR STAR MOTHER

During World War II many homes placed a small flag in the front window and the number of stars in the flag denoted the number of members that family had in military service. A mother with two children in the service carried a flag with two stars, and three stars meant that three members of that family were in the service. My mother was a four-star mother as all four of her boys were in the service and all returned safely after the war.

Frank Dabbs, my oldest brother, was drafted before the war started. He was inducted at Ft. Oglethorpe, Ga., assigned to the military police at that location. He quickly rose to the rank of Master Sergeant. He was later transferred to the medical corps and moved to Denver, Colorado. After a short time there he was sent to some place in Pennsylvania. In early 1945, Frank went to Camp Barkley, Tex. and from there to Staten Island, N. Y., and then to Trenton, N. J. - three moves in a very short time.

R. T. was the next oldest. He married soon after the war started and worked for an aircraft factory for a time before being drafted in late 1942 or early 1943. He was inducted at Ft. Oglethorpe, Ga., sent to Miami, Fla. for basic training and assigned to the Air Corps. R. T. was a corporal and most of his military career was spent in Amarillo, Texas and Ardmore, Oklahoma. During the early stages of the war, I was

Frances Dabbs.

Frank as a young soldier in World War II.   *R.T. as a young soldier during World War II.*

classified 3-A because I was working on an essential job with the railroad. My father had a stroke the year before the war started and was partially paralyzed. Everett, my youngest brother, was still living at home after graduating from high school a short time earlier. He was classified 1-A by the Draft Board. I felt like Everett's place was at home since he provided the primary support for our parents. And, he was little brother... not yet 20 years old. I had it all worked out in my mind that if I enlisted, the Draft Board would not take Everett. He could still live at home and provide needed support for the family.

On July 7, 1942 I wrote the Draft Board and requested that I be placed in 1-A so I could enlist. I enlisted in the Naval Air Corps on Aug. 4, 1942. My strategy to keep my younger brother out of the service failed and Everett was drafted near the end of 1942. He was sent to Camp Robinson, Arkansas.

At Camp Robinson, Everett took his basic training, crawled through dust and hiked miles and miles. When his buddies could not carry their gear, he carried it for them. On October 20, 1943, Everett was in New York headed overseas. He was assigned to the Medical Corps and went overseas in a very small boat. German subs were all around and it was a rough trip. All of the guys got sea sick except for him and he fed them when they were able to eat. Food was very scarce. When they got to England, they received eggs for breakfast and Everett was said to have eaten a dozen.

The English, Americans and French were combining headquarters, and the men were all tested. Later, Everett was in the barracks when he got a call that they were sending a jeep for him to come to London to take some more tests, which he did. Because of his high test scores, he was put in Supreme Headquarters, Allied Expeditionary Force, G-2 Intelligence Division. He received a Certificate of Merit for Outstanding Performance of Duty in G-2. He was then sent to Portsmouth where they slept in tents. One night during an air raid, a piece of shrapnel came through the tent and lodged in the ground next to his head. General Walter Bedell Smith asked for Sgt. Dabbs to keep the war map the day of the invasion, June 6, 1944. When the Allies gained a foothold in France, Everett and his group were flown by bomber across the English Channel. They flew very low because anti aircraft fire was all around them. They set up offices all across France along with the troops until they finally reached Berlin.

Everett hated seeing all of the destruction and all of the hungry children. He often gave the children his food.

When Everett was in Paris, he ran into his first cousin on the street one night. His cousin had sustained a leg wound in the Battle of the Bulge and was on leave. When the Allies arrived in Berlin, Everett and two of his comrades were billeted in a nice apartment. On another occasion , Everett got a three-day pass and visited the Alps in Austria.

Everett was a Staff Sergeant and up for promotion to Master Sergeant when the war ended. He elected to go home before the paper work was completed.

During an air raid one night in London, Everett jumped into a bomb shelter. After a short wait, he felt the need for a cigarette. He punched the soldier next to him and said, "Buddy, you got a light? It turned out that his comrade in the dark was General Eisenhower.

Everett Dabbs.

A FRIEND TO THE SOLDIERS

During World War II most soldiers knew their destination when moving from one military base to another. This was not always true, however, and particularly for soldiers moving in a war zone. I moved 18 times during the war and I knew my destination every time but once.

I was stationed in Miami, Fla. in early 1944. We had completed our training there and were told that we would be leaving the next day, destination unknown. Someone asked if we should wear summer clothes or winter clothes and we were told to wear winter uniforms.

We then conjured up all sorts of expectations as to our destination somewhere in cold country. The following day our contingent of soldiers boarded the train with thoughts of ice and snow on our minds. This wasn't such a happy thought since we had been enjoying the surf in back of our hotel at Miami Beach.

The train departed on time and two hours later we arrived in the small town of Sebring, FL., 90 miles north of Miami. Our destination was Hendricks Field at Sebring which was a bomber base. We were assigned there to wait our turn for flying school.

We were assigned to various departments around the field, mostly to observe. We also caught KP (kitchen police) duty while there and this was the only time I ever had that duty while in Cadet training. While there I peeled potatoes once and worked on the mess serving line a couple of times.

Sebring, FL. was located in central Florida on the shores of Lake Jackson. Orange groves were all around town and you could walk along the streets and pick oranges right off the trees.

A couple of times, on Sunday, my friends and I went into town and spent the day at Lake Jackson. One Sunday, we noticed a big home near the shore of the lake with a couple of boats in the yard. Not being bashful, we decided to ask if we could borrow one of the boats.

We went to the house and rang the bell. A lady came to the door and we told her we were in town from Hendricks Field and we wondered if we might borrow a boat.

She was such a gracious lady and not only let us take a boat, oars and cushions, but insisted that we take fishing rods and reels. Some people were so nice to young men in service during the war and she certainly was one of those special people.

My friends and I spent the day on the lake, got sun-burned, caught only one fish, and we returned all of our equipment in good condition.

I remained in Sebring, Fla. only two months before being sent to Wofford College in Spartanburg, S. C.

THE BOMBARDIER

Denton Dabbs was born in Chattanooga, Tenn., graduated from high school in 1937, and was working for the railroad in Cincinnati, Ohio when the Japanese struck Pearl Harbor in December of 1941.

Southern Railway sponsored a railroad battalion and I knew most of the officer personnel in that unit. I had made up my mind to leave the railroad, take a vacation of one week, and then enlist in the U. S. Amy and ask to be transferred into the 727th Railroad Battalion. While I was on vacation I decided that there would be considerable risk that the army might not transfer me to the railroad battalion once I had enlisted and then I would be at their mercy to assign me wherever they pleased. By the time my vacation was over, I had decided to try to get in the Naval Air Corps, which sounded pretty exciting to me at that time.

On August 4. 1942, I went to Columbus, Ohio to take the physical and mental exams to see if I could qualify for pilot training in the Navy. The tests lasted for two days, following which seven of us were sworn in the United States Naval Reserve. There were fifty young men there to be tested, but only seven of us survived the difficult tests. I then returned to Cincinnati to await my call to active duty.

After several months of waiting, on December 3, 1942 1 was notified that I would be assigned to CPT (Civilian Pilot Training) at the University of Cincinnati. This particular phase of training was part of a Navy V-5 Program.

On December 10th, I received orders to be in Detroit, Michigan not later than 6PM on December 12th. In Detroit, I received a physical, filled out some papers, and returned to Cincinnati on December 13th to begin the CPT program.

The following article appeared in the college paper and pretty well describes the CPT program.

Mis-named C.P.T. Men Live, Learn, Play At U.C.

BY MARY LINN DEBECK

Sequestered in an out-of-the-way barracks in Hanna Hall under the impressive seal of C.P.T., and wearing dapper, dark-green uniforms, is a group of 26 good-natured, fundamentally seriously-minded and thoroughly busy young American men. There are 18 Navy men and eight Army men. All maintain that they are not really the C.P.T. (Civilian Pilot Training) but the W.T.S. (War Training Service). The Navy men likewise proclaim that the Army men are a "purely local outfit." The Navy men are on active duty and receive $75 monthly; the Army men receive no pay.

"Hurry Up, Then Wait"

Not particularly complaining, but just remarking, they comment that they do everything "on the double." Their slogan is "Hurry up and then wait."

Their schedule, to say the least, is full. Up at 6:30 a.m., they straighten up the barracks, wash, and have breakfast in the Union Building, arriving at their first class, military code, at 7:30 a.m. Then they hurry to the Men's Gym to drill, for a half hour. At 10 a.m. they leave by special bus for the airport, where they study and fly until 5:30 p.m. Back at U.C. they take supper and attend class from 7:10 till 9:30 p.m. three nights a week, till 10 p.m. two nights a week.

Two Evenings Free

Saturday and Sunday evenings they have free, and an occasional Friday evening. They have their Sunday meals at Shipley's, which they term their mecca. Breakfasts and suppers they have in the Union Cafeteria; their lunches are packed. Their sanitary facilities are in McMicken and the Men's Gym.

The men seem fairly well satisfied with their lot—at least they don't object—they say that they have "good instructors, good courses, good food, everything good, except the weather." One of a group in the McMicken Commons slyly remarked, "We'd like to remain here for the duration."

They seem to have a good time among themselves, apparently all being close friends. Of course, the Army men, being in the minority, are considered black sheep. The men have an "ants" game in which they all seem to delight, though they will not divulge details of said game.

Mostly College Men

The question of their social relations with others on campus? They've been invited to and attended several Evening College dances and the Interfraternity Dance of Saturday, Feb. 6. They complain, perhaps jokingly, of the lack of liquor. The men mix well with U.C. groups because they are mostly college men themselves.

The group contacted for this story included William (Errol) Flynn, who had two years at a Canadian college; Allan Martin, two years at U.C.; Philip Renener, Ohio State; Pat Donovan, Xavier, '38 (!); William McDaniels; and Harry Metzel, two years at U.C.

They all wished their 'phone number published—though they claim Robert Hetzel (formerly of U.C.) monopolizes it—so here is the number of the phone nearest their impromptu barracks: AV. 9256.

Stearman NS-1 U.S. Navy trainer.

The airport referred to in the article was actually a cornfield on the outskirts of town. Winters can be rather rough in Cincinnati , as they were that year, and flight training was frequently delayed because of heavy snow and a muddy field. I soloed on Feb. 15, 1943, checked out of Stage B on March 3rd, did solo stalls and spins on March 9th. Training was completed on March 25th and I went home to Chattanooga on leave.

I received orders from the Navy on April 17th to report to Detroit on April 20th. In Detroi,./t I received my assignment and left for the University of Iowa for pre-flight training on April 21st. I arrived Iowa City at 8PM. During the next three months we received extensive schooling and an abundance of physical training at the university, which had been taken over by the Navy.

In addition to school our training included extensive swimming tests. We also had a very difficult obstacle course to run and were required to improve our time each week - the penalty for failure to improve was restriction for the week end. We had a 10-mile hike, usually every Saturday morning, and we had to double tine up most hills. For sports, which were rotated on a weekly basis, we had gym and basketball, wrestling and swimming, boxing and soccer, hand to hand combat and football. Our uniforms were the same as those worn by Navy officers, except we were Cadets.

I finished my pre-flight training and on July 7th I was notified that I would be leaving for Minneapolis, Minn. for Primary Flight Training. I left

Iowa City on July l3th at 9PM and arrived Minneapolis at l0AM the next morning.

I had my first flight in the Stearman on July 19th and another flight the following day. On July 28th I was grounded with an ear infection. I continued in ground school but was still grounded on August 6th, which was the anniversary date of my first year in the Navy. On August 9th I started flying again but was somewhat behind other cadets in flight time. I passed MY "A" check on August l3th and had three hours of solo flying on August l4th.

By this time the Navy had so many pilots and so many cadets in training that they really had no place to put them. Cadets were being washed out for any small infraction of the rules. A new law was passed by Congress requiring that any cadet who washed out of flight training would be required to stay in the Navy. All cadets already in flight training were given the option of staying in the Navy under the new guide lines or they could resign as provided under the old guidelines. Several of us went to the Amy Air Corps recruiting office and we were assured that we would be able to pick up in the Amy Air Corps where we left off in the Navy. The prospect of becoming a seaman at some point in time was not too promising to me. Across the country there were a great many cadets who resigned at that time. I requested my discharge on August 17th.

On August 23rd I left for Great Lakes Naval Station near Chicago and arrived that night. I was offered Yeoman's rating to stay in the Navy but declined. On September 2nd I received my discharge from the Naval Reserve. I spent a few days in Rockford, Ill. visiting a friend who had washed out of pilot training, and arrived home in Chattanooga on September 8th.

On September 30th I went to Atlanta, Ga. to take the exams for the Army Air Corps. I passed the exams on October 2nd and

Primary Flight School.

Stewart Field. Newburgh, New York.

Denton as a young Navy Air Cadet in World War II.

returned to Chattanooga. I then went back to Atlanta on October 7th for my physical exam. On November 27th I reported to Ft. Oglethorpe, Ga. to be sworn in the Army Air Corps. On December 2nd I received orders to leave for Camp Shelby, Miss. on December 13th. I arrived in Hattiesburg, Miss. on the morning of December 14th and reported to Camp Shelby. After several days of processing I left Camp Shelby on Dec. 19th and arrived in Miami, Fla. on December 21, 1943. The Air Corps had taken over the hotels at Miami Beach and I was assigned to the Shorecrest Hotel, right on the ocean front.

After several weeks of basic training, physicals, drill, testing, lectures, etc. I was classified as being qualified for pilot, bombardier or navigation training.

I left Miami on February 10, 1944 and moved to Hendricks Field at Sebring, Fla. By this time the Army Air Corps had more cadets than they knew what to do with, and our group was assigned to a waiting pool working in different departments around the field. One hundred cadets were transferred from our group to the infantry on April 3rd.

On April 16th I left for

Wofford College at Spartanburg, S. C. and arrived the following day. After one week the Air Corps realized I had already received this type of schooling while in the Navy so I was moved to Courtland, Ala. on April 25th. Courtland was another waiting pool much like Sebring, Fla. had been.

On June 26th I was transferred to Maxwell Field at Montgomery, Ala. for pre-flight training, much the same as I had received at Iowa City while in the Navy. We had ground school and extensive physical training, ran the obstacle course, spent time in the pressure chamber, and were tested and evaluated. On July 26th I was classified for pilot training. On August 21st I went in the hospital with ptomaine poisoning and remained there until August 29th.

On September 8th 200 of us left for Decatur, Ala. to begin Primary Flight Training. Our regular schedule consisted of half day on the flight line and half day for classes, drill and physical training. We had two classes a day and subjects covered were engines, navigation, aircraft and Naval recognition, theory of flight, code and lectures on other subjects. After two hours in class we had one hour of physical training and one hour of drill. We had a five mile cross country run twice a week. Our flight instructors were civilian and our planes were Stearman PT-17's, a neat little biplane with a 220 HP engine. We were given only one flight a day until we soloed. We had been there about three weeks when we were told our primary training was to be extended five extra weeks. This meant 15 weeks instead of 10. About 30% of our class failed to make it through primary. By December 16th I had 90 hours of flying in the PT-17. On December 18th fifteen of us were selected to go to Stewart Field in New York for basic training. Our class was to be an experimental class flying AT-6's in Basic Training and B-25's in Advanced Training.

I left Decatur on Dec. 21st with a delay enroute before reporting to Stewart Field. I returned to Chattanooga and was married on December 22, 1944. On December 30th I left for Stewart Field. The weather was extreme and we had a big snow every few days. It was difficult to get in regular flying time as the snow along the runways was piled higher than the wing tips of the planes. I felt that my instructor was indifferent about being an instructor as he was being reassigned in a few weeks. We spent most of our time just flying around as the auxiliary fields were not suitable to practice take offs and landings. I did not solo in the required time and was subject to being washed out of pilot training. I was put on report and when I later

Flew this plane during training in New York.

Big Spring, Texas. AT-11. October 1945.

received a check ride with the top officer he told me there was nothing wrong with my flying. Unfortunately, by this time, I had fallen behind the remainder of the class and I was washed out. The record showed, so I was told, "personality clash with instructor". On January 29th, 1945 1 was given furlough until Feb. 11th. At that time I was reclassified for Bombardier training and left for Moody Field, Ga. on Feb. 14th.

I was only at Moody Field in Valdosta, Ga. for a very short time

Army Air Corps Cadet in Miami, FL.

before being sent to Maxwell Field in Montgomery, Ala. on March 12th. On April 1st I left for Big Spring, Texas for Bombardier Training, arriving there on April 4th. Four men in our barracks were killed in a night crash on April 22nd. I had my first flight in the twin engine bomber, AT-11, on April 30th. For the next several months we went through extensive ground school training, practice bombing missions over targets in the desert, and cross country flights in navigation. When Japan signed formal surrender on Sept. 2nd, I had two flights remaining before graduation from Bombardier School, and receiving my wings as an officer in the Amy Air Corps. There was some doubt that we would be allowed to finish since the war was over. We were first told that we would not finish, then we were told we could graduate if we would sign up for three more years of service. Then, finally, we were allowed to finish and go home on furlough. I graduated and earned my silver wings as Flight Officer on September 19, 1945. At that tine I was given a 15 day furlough and went home to Chattanooga. When I returned to Big Spring, I was given the option of signing up for three more years of duty, with probably assignment overseas, or being discharged. I elected to be discharged. I was ordered to report to Barksdale Field in Shreveport, La. and received my discharge on Oct. 26, 1945.

Following the war I applied for entry in the 727th Railroad Battalion (Reserve) and was appointed Adjutant with the rank of First Lieutenant. I served in this capacity for six years before receiving my final discharge

TURNING THE TIDE

After the Japanese struck Pearl Harbor in December of 1941, the nation committed itself to the war and the year 1942 became a period of change.

Men, and a few women, were mobilized into the armed service. The entire population found a role in production or civil defense... or both. The sale of new cars or trucks was banned, sugar was rationed and gasoline rationing coupons were issued.

Defense plants and ship yards went on 24 hours a day; the nation went on daylight savings time, called War Time, and the minimum draft age was lowered from 21 to 18 years of age.

The Philippines were lost, as was the Bataan Peninsula. Because of the fear that the Japanese would invade California, 110,000 Americans of Japanese ancestry were relocated in special camps for detention.

Japan's plans to invade Australia were foiled when its forces were intercepted in the Coral Sea. The Japanese attempted to take Midway Island and lost a critical battle.

U. S. Marines landed on Guadalcanal, but it would be early 1943 before the island was completely under U. S. control.

U. S. bombers made their first raid on Europe in August, and in November the allied forces landed in French North Africa. The first air raid on Italy was made in December. So, by the end of the year 1942, the Allies were beginning to strike back, the armed forces were mobilized and supplies were flowing from factories across the land.

In 1943 the tide began to turn as Allied forces around the world went on the offensive.

The postal service in 1993 issued a number of stamps commemorating 1943: Turning the Tide. It was an issue of 10 stamps around a map of the world - and the map listed many of the events that led to turning the tide.

The stamps revived memories that for me seemed not so long ago. In the Pacific, the Allies were active in the Solomon Islands, the Gilbert Islands, Tarawa, New Guinea and the Aleutians. North Africa was taken, Sicily and Italy were invaded and Allied bombers began their raids on German targets, though they sustained heavy losses.

The war would go on for many more months, but 1943 was the beginning of Turning the Tide.

THE FIRST ATOMIC BOMBS

On August 6, 1945 the eyes of the world were exposed for the first time to the horrors of the atomic bomb. On that date the United States dropped an atomic bomb on the Japanese city of Hiroshima. The bomb leveled about four square miles of the city and killed between 80,000 and 140,000 people.

Three days later a second bomb was dropped on the city of Nagasaki, causing less destruction because the city was more spread out.

On August 14th the Japanese decreed its surrender to the Allies, thus ending World War II. Those bombs did what the United States hoped they would do - end the war with Japan.

Ruins of Church in Nagasaki, 1946.

I suppose history will ultimately pass judgment on the morality of dropping such a bomb on a helpless city, but there was little sympathy for the Japanese people at that time. There was great hatred of the Japanese for their unprovoked attack on Pearl Harbor on Dec. 7, 1941, at which time they sank most of the American fleet at anchor and killed some 2500 people with their bombs. And thousands more U. S. military personnel were killed in the subsequent years leading up to Aug. 6, 1945.

By 1945 the United States had started preparations for the invasion of Japan and it was estimated that thousands of more lives would be lost by the Allies in such an invasion. The Japanese had said they were prepared to give up 10 million lives to protect their homeland. So, while the atomic bombs that were dropped on Japan killed a lot of people, they probably prevented the loss of life for thousands more, and especially the lives of our young men.

At the time the first atomic bomb was dropped, my three brothers and I were in the service of our country. My youngest brother was in Berlin with General Eisenhower. One of my brothers was stationed in New Jersey and the other was in Oklahoma. As for me, I was stationed at an air base in Texas, and rumor had us slated for the South Pacific in just a few weeks.

I never knew how my brothers felt about the atomic bomb ending the war. For me, the atomic bomb meant the end of the war and I could go home - I suspect they felt the same way too.

GOING HOME

I have traveled quite a bit in my lifetime and there are a few places that will always remain in my memory. I remember the tranquil beauty of Prince Edward Island in Canada and the rugged shore of Newfoundland. I remember the beauty of Zion National Park and Bryce Canyon National Park in Utah and the Grand Canyon in Arizona. I remember the quaint little village on Tangier Island in the middle of Chesapeake Bay where there were no automobiles.

I remember all of these beautiful places but there is one memory of a sight I will always cherish, not only for the beauty but the feelings associated with it.

The year was 1945. I had been in military service for three years during which time I had seen a few sights, both on the ground and from the air. I had traveled quite a few miles during those years, to many large cities and numerous small towns where air bases were located. I had been moved seventeen times in those three years - all places dull and drab, devoid of heart and soul.

With the ending of the war I was sent to Shreveport to receive my discharge from the Army Air Corps. With the paper work completed, I headed home to Chattanooga, Tenn.

As the train came out of the tunnel through Lookout Mountain, I could see the city nestled there in the valley on the banks of the Tennessee River. Down below was the bond in the river, known as Moccasin Bend, and in the distance was Signal Mountain.

I thought it was the most beautiful sight I had ever seen. It was familiar territory for my eyes and I was floating on air. The war was really over - I was heading home. It was not just a dream - there was the river and the mountains and the city I knew so well. I grew up there and it was home.

Going home - that was what it was all about. Going home to Ann... to mom and dad, my brothers... the people I loved and who loved me.

The valley had never seemed so beautiful before, but on that day it was the most beautiful place in all the world.

Tennessee River.

Aviation Cadet William C. Wheat, killed while in training.

Capt. Herbert C. Davis, killed in a plane crash in New Mexico.

First Lt. James R. Crockett, P-51 fighter pilot, shot down over Germany.

Lt. Edward T. Wilson, B-26 bomber pilot, shot down over Italy.

(Top Left) Victor Culberson, reported killed in action.

(Top Right) Lt. David O. Schoocraft, reported killed.

(Above Left) Ensign James Campbell, crashed off the coast of Florida. (Above Right) Lt. William C. Williams, Bombardier, shot down over Austria.

(Left) Lt. Jack Clark, Bombardier, shot down over Germany.

Lt. T.E. Hale, fighter pilot, killed in a crash in England.

First Lt. Kenneth D. Hicks, shot down over Germany.

Staff Sgt. Lawrence S. Medlin, killed in a bomber crash in Arizona.

Staff Sgt. Sam B. Henry, killed in Belgium.

First Lt. Travis Moore, bomber pilot, shot down over Truk in the pacific.

(Left) Lt. Roy E. Thomas, pilot, last reported on Corregidor and Bataan.

INDEX

Printed in the USA
CPSIA information can be obtained
at www.ICGtesting.com
JSHW021834311023
51203JS00004B/65

9 781681 623993